I0212239

TURNING POINT

Love & Obey Female Led

Affirmations

Marisa Rudder

© 2020 Marisa Rudder.

All rights reserved.

No part of this publication may be reproduced, distributed, or transmitted in any form or by any means, including photocopying, recording, or other electronic or mechanical methods, without the prior written permission of the publisher, except in the case of brief quotations embodied in critical reviews and certain other noncommercial uses permitted by copyright law. For permission requests, write to the author below.

All of Marisa Rudder's Bestselling Books are available on Amazon: *Love & Obey, Real Men Worship Women, Oral Sex For Women, Cuckolding, Spanking, Chastity,* and *Turning Point*.

Please contact Marisa Rudder with any questions:

Email: femaleledrelationshipbook@gmail.com

Printed in the United States of America Publisher's Cataloging-in-Publication data

ISBN: 978-1-7361835-1-9

Dedication

I would like to dedicate this book to all the strong, brave ladies who have joined or about to join the Love & Obey movement and live a female led lifestyle and the supportive gentlemen who recognized the natural superiority of females. It is also my desire that women and men experience the joy, happiness, and passion from exploring all aspects of a loving Female Led Relationship (FLR) and understanding all the benefits of a loving female authority. If you have not already, please join us on social media. You can find out more at our website: www.loveandobey.com, or follow me on social media:

FACEBOOK
https://www.facebook.com/femaleledrelationships

TWITTER
https://twitter.com/loveandobeybook

INSTAGRAM
https://www.instagram.com/femaleledrelationships

WARNING

This book contains adult sexual content. It should not be read by anyone under the age of 18 years. In addition to sexually explicit and descriptive content, this book contains controversial sexual discussions about spanking, discipline, and Female Led Relationships.

Introduction

The spoken word has been one of the greatest instruments of change. Words have the ability to motivate, inspire, and transform. Great speakers and their memorable speeches will be remembered for decades to come, like Winston Churchill, Martin Luther King, Jr., John F. Kennedy, and Ronald Reagan. Evangelists like Joel Osteen and motivational speakers like Anthony Robbins have all created movements and even paradigm shifts in society with their words. Affirmations have become a powerful method in creating change in an individual's life and now in relationships.

The world is becoming female led and Female Led Relationships are growing. More couples are switching to a Female Led Relationship and my *Love and Obey* movement has helped to promote and expand awareness of female empowerment. A Female Led Relationship is one in which the female leads and makes the decisions, and her man is the supportive gentleman who follows. Relationships can be challenging to maneuver, but it becomes even more challenging when attempting to transition to a new type of partnership.

When men decide to submit fully to their Queen, the desire is strong and is often the driving force for Female Led Relationships, but settling into daily life and countering past conditioning can be an issue for many men. There can be a constant battle. Patriarchal thinking and rigid gender roles can prevent some men from being able to be their best in an FLR. When men can fully commit and follow their Queen's lead, then all is well. He experiences tremendous relief, and he is generally much happier.

Many couples experience resistance during the transition from patriarchal to female led. People in relationships will experience many adjustments. The true test of dealing with change is how couples choose to address these changes and work through them. There are some changes that commonly occur, which can make or break a relationship. Change in life is always challenging and even more difficult when it involves your relationship, which is an important glue that holds the two of you and your family together.

Today, there has never been more pressure and stress with all of the responsibilities and factors that affect you and your

Queen, but holding it together and being in unity as a couple or family is even more crucial. The relationship can be a real source of stability during chaotic times. What I recognized years ago was that a Female Fed Relationship works because the Queen assumes the position as leader and the man is the supportive gentleman. Roles are clearly defined and leadership is established. This type of relationship can offer increased intimacy, connectedness, and communication. But it requires complete submission by the man, and often men must make the ultimate sacrifice to change everything they were conditioned to believe from youth.

How do men make this transition? First, my six books in the *Love and Obey* series offers all of the rules and instructions to help you and your Queen learn almost everything there is to know about creating the perfect Female Led Relationship or marriage. A relationship is like a ship, and it must be carefully steered in the right direction to be successful. Affirmations have the power to create a turning point in your life and your relationship.

I am here to help you be successful, and my books give you everything you need to create the best Female Led Relationship or wife-led marriage. But now, I take it a step further. *Love and Obey* affirmations are going to help you to completely reprogram your mind and past patriarchal conditioning. After diving into this book and putting it into practice each and every day, you are going to release the old, stodgy, limited thinking that is limiting your potential and stifling progress in your female led goals.

Neuroplasticity is the ability of the brain to continuously create new neural pathways. When we repeat a skill that we are trying to master or words as in affirmations, we strengthen the neural networks that represent such action. The same happens physically in the brain whether we perform the action or simply visualize it. Self-affirmation theory and practice has shown real positive outcomes and has transformed the lives of many in areas like health, wealth, happiness, and now relationships.

You will be required to practice your affirmations daily, so it becomes ingrained. I am confident that you will begin to experience the effects of this powerful tool in your life and your relationship in no time. Your Queen will be singing your praises in the morning and excited to jump into bed for another sexual adventure once you have fully committed to her pleasure. You will be excited to be in service to her and place her on a pedestal, and she will reward you with the best sex, more excitement, and adventure than you dreamed of.

Only a couple who has turned inward and is crazy for each other can take the relationship to new heights. We always think that the answer to more fun lies outside with friends and new acquaintances, but in fact, a relationship that has grown deeper is far more inspiring and fulfilling. Happiness can be found in a Female Led Relationship, which is where she is indeed your true Queen and you submit to her 100 percent. *Love and Obey* affirmations will help transform your thinking. You will be excited to try all of the tips and tricks explained throughout this book and you will have a clear understanding of how to fully pleasure your Queen. Pleasure is mind and body.

Albert Einstein once said, "Imagination is more important than knowledge." So, how do you imagine your perfect relationship? Affirmations help you to add the power mental aspect and take your relationship to a whole new level. Your Queen is the human embodiment and expression of divine feminine energy. Come on this journey of exploration with me into *Love and Obey* affirmations, and watch your life and relationship transition from boring and mundane to exciting and adventurous.

Marisa Rudder

Table of Contents

CHAPTER 1

Love and Obey Affirmations and the Relationship

Female Led Relationships are growing—there is no question. More women are taking charge in every aspect of life, and men love being the supportive gentleman. The *Love and Obey* movement teaches that female led authority can be loving and nurturing while placing the woman in the rightful position as Queen. The divorce rate sits at about 50 percent, and I believe that we are on the cusp of a revolution when there are more female led marriages and relationships, and not only will there be a decrease in divorces, but there will be an increase in well-being and internal happiness in both and women.

Today, there are examples of female leadership growing in countries, governments, corporations, and now the home. In the USA, the first female Vice President was elected when 200 years ago women were unable to even vote. The number of women who are the primary breadwinners in their families is on the rise. According to a 2018 research from the U.S. Census Bureau, one in four heterosexual married couples reveals that women make more than their male partners.

The Female Led Relationship gives women the opportunity to take charge in the home. Men have reported more happiness because they have witnessed increased intimacy and sexual pleasure serving a woman who is ready to take charge. Women are happier because they are treated as the Queen, and they receive the support they need in a focused, caring, supportive man. In the female led world, there are responsibilities on both sides. Women must step up and assume the leadership role while men must be willing to submit completely and follow her lead.

One of the biggest issues that can arise in relationships is the transition. How can men really learn to do something if they feel it may go against their nature? You've been taught to take control and "be a man," be strong and assertive all of your life, and now, with times changing and a desire to serve your Queen, you must adapt and change. I recognized a long time ago that real change in relationships can be the most difficult undertaking. Even therapy without practicing the principles learned can result in failure.

Have you ever come across a strong woman who seemed perfect relationship material but after a few dates, you could tell that you just didn't feel the same level of attraction as you felt originally for her? And you really wanted to take things to the next level, but for some reason, you can't seem to show a similar intention and you didn't know what to do about it? Or do you often struggle to keep her interest for long? Have you ever slept with a woman too soon only to realize that she has almost disappeared from your life for no apparent reason? And does it happen a lot even when you know it shouldn't be happening? Or are you in a relationship where you just don't know how to commit further and take it to the next level? And you always ask yourself: Why isn't my relationship moving forward?

Every time you think about this subject you want to avoid dealing with it because it makes you even more distant and withdrawn to the point where you fear your Queen might leave you? Are you feeling absolutely helpless and frustrated because you want to make her understand how much you want to be with her? You could be holding yourself back with past conditioning and making it impossible to relax and enjoy your new Female Led Relationship.

This is where *Love and Obey* affirmations can create a turning point and provide a real purpose. After you have fully immersed yourself by reading all of my other books in the

Love and Obey collection, you are now ready to take the plunge and change your life. It is time to make service to your Queen a priority by changing your thinking and conditioning with these daily affirmations. I recognized a long time ago, after writing my second book *Real Men Worship Women,* that men need rules to follow in order to create the right relationship groundwork and to get through the transition.

If men understand these rules early on, then there will be less conflict, stress, and anxiety in the transition stage. This transition is the period when a man may desire change, but he must also change his way of thinking, which has been ingrained in him from young. Properly worshipping the Queen requires reprogramming at the subconscious level, along with following all of the rules daily. When a man has achieved reprogramming, the woman is going to feel more confident and relaxed. Both you and your Queen can be relaxed. Once you have reprogrammed your patriarchal thinking, it will be easier to address the Queen as supreme.

Speech is important in Female Led Relationships. A man must obey his woman in his speech, calling her Goddess, Queen, or Mistress. "Yes, Queen, of course, my Goddess." "As you command, my Queen." By adding speech in the form of affirmations to worship her daily, you are able to change past conditioning. Female led will become as normal as brushing your teeth and flossing. The more ingrained a female led life is in men, the less disagreements and the more opportunity to create a deeper more intimate connection.

However, the breakdown occurs when women and men are unsure of their roles and this struggle can exist when couples focus overly on "equality" in a relationship. There is no equality in governments or organizations and rarely is it achieved in relationships. How often does anything get accomplished if everyone in the firm is equal and there is no leader? Usually never. The same is true in relationships. Women have allowed themselves to believe that the best they can hope for is equality. The pursuit of equality eventually leads to disagreement and power struggles.

At some point, one person needs to step up and take the lead. For years, that was expected to be the man, but today, in a Female Led Relationship, the Queen needs to take leadership in making the decisions and managing the day-to-day activities in the relationship. There is a reason the saying, "Happy Wife, Happy Life" exists. When the Queen is happy, you as the supportive gentleman, will be happy too. The challenge occurs when a man must change his thinking on a deeper level.

Perhaps you are just discovering female led life but you have been conditioned to be patriarchal. Many men are raised by women, but having divorced parents tend to affect how men will view their position in relationships. Men may have a desire to submit, but desire and doing this daily with their Queens can be problematic. This is where reprogramming comes in and affirmations can be beneficial.

Affirmations are used to reprogram the subconscious mind, to encourage us to believe certain things about ourselves or about the world and our place within it. They are also used to help us create the reality we want. *Love and Obey* affirmations will help you through this transition. You will reprogram much of your old ways of thinking, and you can practice these affirmations at any time. In the morning, during sex, or during a meditative break. Female led affirmations are designed to help you get rid of the chains of the old patriarchal conditioning that often prevents men from being truly present in their relationships.

This book presents a great opportunity for both you and your Queen to become even more intimate. To be effective, you must both set aside all other distractions and focus on doing these affirmations in a time set aside for you to be together. Consistent practice yields great results, and the more you commit to following *Love and Obey* affirmations, the faster you will notice changes in your thinking and accepting of female led life. There is lots of science and research that support and demonstrate the power of affirmations, so much that it has become an essential tool along with meditation, mindfulness training, and many other mental and spiritual practices for helping couples.

Affirmations have been an essential component in wealth, health, stress, manifesting, and change on a much deeper level. I believe that *Love and Obey* affirmations will become an extremely powerful program for taking you and your Queen to a whole new level in Female Led Relationships, and it will help to reprogram limiting patriarchal conditioning.

CHAPTER 2

What are Affirmations?

Affirmations are becoming more popular, and they have seen significant use in many aspects of mental reprogramming for health, stress management, well-being, and now relationships. Affirmations seem simple on the surface—just repeat a couple of lines, but they are, in fact, a powerful method to control specific areas of the brain that can bring about great transformation. Many gurus and spiritual leaders swear by affirmations, and they have become an important part of many programs. For hundreds of years, the wisdom teachings of the East have utilized methods for the study and transformation of the mind-body. Mindfulness Training provides instruction in meditation, mind-body healing, and affirmations from both a psychological and spiritual perspective. Reprogramming is real and can be used in relationships.

The Female Led Relationship is powerful, but for many couples, there are challenges when a man must transition to his new role of supportive gentleman. Men have varying degrees of success with getting through this transition; however, many encounter difficulties when they must get to the deeper levels of serving their Queens. *Love and Obey* affirmations are designed to help you through these transitions.

I recognized many years ago that men were major supporters of female led life. More men would contact me on a daily basis requesting guidance on how to create a better Female Led Relationship. However, they were also the ones who expressed difficulty with fully committing and showing submission. I realized that one of the greatest achievements would be to help men with their transition from patriarchal thinking to female led life. *Love and Obey* affirmations are yet another tool that can help men with their desire to serve. The more you can align your mental desire to serve with action, the more success you will have in your Female Led Relationship. Most women are already chomping at the bit and eager to take charge. Many couples experience some growing pains when the female is demanding proper service from her man, but men are not completely capable of submitting to her. Yes, it can take some time to adjust, or it takes fully immersing yourself in learning to love, obey, and serve her.

Neuroscience shows us that every minute of every day, our body is physically changing in response to the thoughts that run through our head. Just thinking about something causes your brain to send signals and release neurotransmitters. These chemicals control virtually all of your body's functions, including your mood and feelings. Over time and with repetition, via neuroplasticity, it's been proven that your thoughts change your brain, your cells, and even your genes. What you think, visualize, and say to yourself can change your body, brain, and life.

One way to harness this power to help you is through affirmations. Studies suggest that positive affirmations can help us respond in a less defensive and resistant way when presented with life challenges. For example, a significant challenge is changes in the relationship. When men attempt to live out their fantasy with a strong demanding woman, they need guidance and instruction on how to navigate their new purpose of submitting and serving their Queen. My books *Love and Obey* and *Real Men Worship Women* provided the rules and general instructions on how to properly worship the Queen.

Now, *Love and Obey* affirmations will help to make this instruction much more natural as it becomes a part of your normal thinking. You will no longer be drawn to patriarchal tendencies, but rather, you will begin to think as a fully supportive gentleman. The reason this is so powerful is because subconscious, ingrained conditioning can surface and affect your behavior in relationships. The more you can reprogram your mind to serve your Queen and view her as supreme, the fewer conflicts will arise and this translates into more happiness in your relationship.

Affirmations were made popular by gurus like Napoleon Hill, the author of *Think and Grow Rich*, who went on to sell millions of copies of his self-help programs. Most of his books were promoted as expounding principles to achieve "success." Another extremely successful book and program that uses affirmations is *The Secret,* which promoted "the Law of Attraction" using affirmations. It was so successful it has sold over 30 million copies worldwide and translated into 50 languages. There is no doubt that affirmations change lives, and when used correctly, they will help you and your Queen to create the perfect Female Led Relationship. By directing your thoughts, these affirmations will help put into the vibration for attracting your desires.

The first step in manifesting is to be clear as to what you want. Most people are not able to form a clear concise picture of what they actually truly desire, and this is a necessary step in using affirmations to create the turning point and your new perfect Female Led Relationship. You must visualize what your desired life looks like. Believe it is really happening as you repeat the affirmations. Then you need to trust the process and show gratitude and acceptance for your Queen and your desired new relationship or marriage. Only when careful attention to this is done daily will you witness an amazing transformation.

CHAPTER 3

How Do Affirmations Work?

Self-affirmation theory suggests that people have a fundamental motivation to maintain self-integrity, perceive themselves as good, virtuous, and able to predict and control imperative outcomes. In virtually all cultures and historical periods, there are socially shared conceptions of what it means to be a person of self-integrity. Having self-integrity means that one perceives oneself as living up to a culturally specific conception of goodness, virtue, and agency. Self-affirmation theory examines how people maintain self-integrity when this perception of the self is threatened.

Changing patriarchal conditioning, which has been deeply ingrained for years, can affect self-integrity. Personal regard is related to self-integrity. Researchers have examined the psychology of the importance of people's sense of personal regard. Some have suggested that a sense of personal regard emerges early in an infant's and remains relatively stable throughout the lifetime. They have also documented the various adaptations people deploy to maintain self-regard. The social psychologist Daniel Gilbert and his colleagues have suggested that people have a psychological immune system that initiates psychological adaptations to threats to self-regard.

Indeed, these protective adaptations may lead to rationalizations and even distortions of reality. When self-integrity is threatened, according to self-affirmation theory, people need not defensively rationalize or distort reality. Instead, they can reestablish self-integrity through affirmations. Affirmations are positive statements used to challenge negative, depressing, or anxiety-producing thoughts and beliefs. They can also just be general supportive thoughts providing encouragement. Think of daily affirmations as exercising the mind. Affirmations reinforce an intention so deeply that it bypasses one's conscious mind and goes straight into the subconscious. This is powerful because the subconscious mind believes what it is told, much like a blank screen that displays whatever is projected onto it.

Repeating affirmations helps to reprogram the unconscious mind for success. It helps eliminate negative and limiting beliefs and transforms your comfort zone from a limited one, keeping you trapped in mediocrity to a more expanded one where anything is possible. Affirmations are used to influence your thinking patterns, behavioral habits, health, and moods. Affirmations come out of self-affirmation theory contends that if individuals reflect on values that are personally relevant, they are less likely to experience distress and react defensively when confronted with information that contradicts or threatens their sense of self.

People's attempt to protect self-integrity may threaten the integrity of their relationships with others. Yet, these normal adaptations can be turned off' through a psychological adaptation to threat, an alternative adaptation that does not hinge on distorting the threatening event to render it less significant. One way that these defensive adaptations can be reduced, or even eliminated, is through the process of self-affirmation. This makes them perfect for reprogramming for something as serious as a relationship, which affects so much of our lives.

Affirmations are aligned with Freud's explanation of the conscious mind as the tip of the iceberg with the subconscious and unconscious beneath that allows us to discuss affirmations and their impact on behavioral changes by accessing the subconscious to drive the conscious behavior. Imagine that the subconscious mind is like a computer drive. It sorts every thought, action, and memory, and over time, the drive gets cluttered and the "files" become corrupted, with some files appearing more dominant than others.

In our subconscious mind, these files can relate to negative influences in our environment, messages from powerful authoritarian figures, bad habits we pick up over time, chronic stress, and ingrained habits related to food choices. Positive thinking and the subconscious works with health issues. For one study, cancer survivors reported that participants with higher optimism reported better health, greater happiness, and hopefulness. Affirmations were also found to affect cardiovascular functioning.

At the behavioral level, self-affirmation improves problem-solving performance on tasks related to executive functioning. Numerous studies highlight that thinking about self-preferences activates neural reward pathways. A group of researchers found that self-affirmation would activate brain reward circuitry during functional MRI studies. Their findings suggest that self-affirmation may be rewarding and may provide a first step toward identifying a neural mechanism by which it may produce beneficial effects. By enhancing the psychological resources of self-integrity, the act of self-affirmation reduces defensive responses to threatening information and events, leading to positive outcomes.

Change Unhealthy Conditioning

Many relationships begin to unravel when there is too much unhealthy conditioning happening. For example, you have been together with your partner for a while and have developed poor communication habits. With increasing arguments and disagreements, you both just ignore it. Psychologist Patricia Evans discusses negative conditioning that occurs in relationships. She tells the story of a scientist who uses two frogs to study the effects of conditioning. The scientist places the first frog in a pan of hot water. The frog immediately jumps out. She places the second frog in a pan of cold water while the scientist gradually turns up the heat. The frog doesn't move. The scientist gradually turns up the heat again. The frog continues to stay. The scientist continues to turn up the heat, and yet again, the frog stays. Finally, the scientist turns up the heat to a boiling point. The frog continues to stay until it's boiled to death. This is similar with abuse, which often starts out slowly, and gradually picks up speed and intensity.

Unfortunately, this pattern can continue unending for years and years. Slowly, day by day, a person's soul gets chipped away. One day the person wakes up and realizes he/she has been sitting in a pan of boiling water. The reason conditioning is a powerful part of all relationships is because it can hinder progress, particularly when it is necessary to make major changes in having to create a Female Led Relationship. Affirmations and daily practice can go a long way to changing unhealthy conditioning, and for the Female Led Relationships, patriarchal conditioning.

Why Patriarchal Conditioning Needs to Be Changed

Couple's therapist and bestselling author Terry Real is a member of the senior faculty at the Family Institute of Cambridge and Director of the Gender Relations program at the Meadows Institute in Arizona. Terry Real says, "We all live under patriarchy, which is a rigid dichotomy of gender roles. Traditionally, men are supposed to be strong and feel independent, unemotional, logical and confident. Women are supposed to be expressive, nurturer, weak and dependent. One of the things I say about those traditional gender roles is they don't make anybody happy and they don't make for intimacy." He believes that in order to lead men and women into happiness and intimacy, men and women must be led out of patriarchy since they are old rules not built for intimacy and happiness. He says, "The essence of masculinity is contempt for the feminine. Misogyny and masculinity are flip sides of the same coin. What it means to be a "man" today is to not be a girl. Not be feminine. The contempt for the feminine is part of the patriarchal culture." This leads to more unhealthy relationships, which could be part of the reason why the divorce rate is at 50 percent.

What's worse is that the real origin of patriarchy is not really known. Patriarchy is associated with a set of ideas, a patriarchal ideology that acts to explain and justify this dominance and attributes it to inherent natural differences between men and women. If we truly analyze what men want, patriarchy also fails to fulfill these needs. In a recent study, men described what led to their own divorces, as well as what they most value in a woman. From this, it was concluded that the goal of men is to reduce complexity in their lives and what men want most from women is to feel truly appreciated. It's all about simplicity and appreciation. Female Led Relationships address both of these needs. A strong woman in charge helps to simplify things because she leads and the man follows.

In addition, when a man worships and serves a woman correctly, he will feel appreciated and rewarded. Female Led Relationships are growing because they are congruent with the state of our existence. With women leading, there is much more emphasis on communication and empathy. The world needs more communication in a digital world and not much brute strength. A man can begin to develop his intuitive empathetic side with affirmations with the focus on serving his woman. Not only does this place the focus on his woman daily, but he also retains a goal and purpose in his life.

Meditation and Affirmations Can Go Together

Meditation can make your affirmations more powerful. Try meditating together with your Queen. Make it a light ritual at the beginning of your session to help to center your mind and body. Once you get into meditation and feel connected energetically, notice the subtle sensations you feel in your body. You may feel energized and tingly. Now you can begin to pleasure each other while staying connected to the sensations created by your meditation. Once you are in the zone, you can add your affirmations for an even more powerful experience. Harness sexual energy by moving it. By moving your sexual energy out of your genitals and pelvis, you distribute the pleasure and goodness throughout your entire body. Rather than keeping the pleasure centered in your clitoris or the head of your penis, your whole body vibrates with pleasure.

Here are a few methods to help you start moving your sexual energy. Everything begins with intention. Set the intention to feel the subtle sensations of your sexual energy and move them. If you want the energy to move, it will. This is nothing more than imagining that it's real.

Visualization is another great technique to add. You can use the power of your mind's eye to create something amazing. I recommend visualizing your sexual energy and your pleasure as a ball of white light. You can then imagine it expanding or moving throughout your body.

Next, whatever you focus on, grows. Keep your attention glued to your sexual energy and your pleasure. It's just like meditation. If your mind wanders to a fantasy, or thinking about what you have to do, just gently return it to your sexual energy and where you are moving it to.

Last, your breath is a huge component to great sex generally. But you can also use it to move sexual energy. You can essentially "blow" your energy around your body. Once you are in a relaxed state, you can begin to repeat your *Love and Obey* affirmations, while maintaining this meditative state.

CHAPTER 4

The Power of Affirmations and Neuroscience

Affirmations have been used to create wealth, love, beauty, happiness, and now they will be used to create the perfect Female Led Relationship. According to Walter E. Jacobson, M.D., there is value in affirmations of this nature because our subconscious mind plays a major role in the actualization of our lives and the manifestation of our desires. What we believe about ourselves at a subconscious level, he says, can have a significant impact on the outcome of events. When we feel good about ourselves and have a positive attitude, our lives tend to run more smoothly, with fewer obstacles, less chaos and drama, and greater cooperation and support from others. When we feel bad about ourselves and have a negative attitude, we tend to resist healthy choices, engage in more risky and impulsive behaviors, behave in a variety of self-sabotaging ways and put up walls between ourselves and others. Consequently, affirmations, which program our subconscious mind to aid us in manifesting the destiny we desire, can be very helpful.

When we speak positively of ourselves, we build our self-esteem. When we criticize ourselves, we feel vulnerable. If our inner dialogue is continuously negative, then our emotional state will be negative too. When our body is in a constant state of stress, we're more prone to illness and disease. If, on the other hand, our internal dialogue is positive, then we're likely to feel stronger in our sense of self. As a result, we're more resilient and less threatened by other people's negativity and less defensive in our response, resulting in a much calmer approach to life and living. Dr. Angele Close, PhD, a clinical psychologist and therapist, states, "Shifting our mental attention towards our intention has the potential to help us steer away from negative thinking patterns and create a positive change in mood, mindset, and energy,"

When spoken with conviction, positive self-affirmations can help alter our thoughts, emotions, beliefs, and behavior. The key, however, is to be quite imaginative and to use lots of imagery and visualization. The more real we make what it is we're affirming, the stronger the neural connections become. It helps if we can visualize ourselves as "having," "being" or "doing" what it is we're affirming; this makes it more experiential and more real. If, to begin with, you find this difficult to do, just pretend. Your mind doesn't know the difference between real or pretend. It helps to engage all senses of sight, sound, feel, taste, and smell when stating our affirmations as this helps anchor and lock the affirmation deeper into our subconscious mind.

Research studies show that positive self-affirmation practices can be beneficial in many ways:

1. Self-affirmations can decrease health-deteriorating stress.

2. People have successfully increased their physical activity levels using self-affirmations in experiments.

3. Affirmations have been shown to help people perceive "threatening" messages with less resistance. These results suggest that people can apply self-affirmation as a tool for coping with everyday challenges.

4. Practicing self-affirmation has effectively lowered stress and rumination, both of which contribute to depression and anxiety.

5. Affirmations can significantly increase feelings of hopefulness.

6. In one study, a short affirmation exercise boosted the problem-solving abilities of "chronically stressed" subjects to the same level as those with low stress.

7. Affirmations have been used to successfully treat people with low self-esteem, depression, and other mental health conditions.

8. Evidence suggests that affirmations can help you perform better at work. According to researchers, spending just a few minutes thinking about your best qualities before a high-pressure meeting can calm your nerves, increase your confidence, and improve your chances of a successful outcome.

Affirmations and the Brain

Researchers at the Annenberg School for Communication, in collaboration with researchers at the University of Michigan and UCLA, have uncovered what goes on in our brains during self-affirmations. The study, led by Christopher Cascio and Associate Professor Emily Falk, was published in the journal of *Social Cognitive and Affective Neuroscience*. They reasoned that the brain-activity patterns displayed by people undergoing self-affirmation could provide support for the current, tentative explanations for how the technique works. The study used functional magnetic resonance imaging (fMRI) to find that self-affirmation activates well-known reward centers in the brain. These areas—the ventral striatum and ventromedial prefrontal cortex—are the same reward centers that respond to other pleasurable experiences, such as eating your favorite meal or winning a prize.

"Affirmation takes advantage of our reward circuits, which can be quite powerful," says Cascio. "Many studies have shown that these circuits can do things like dampen pain and help us maintain balance in the face of threats." The study also found that self-affirmation increases activity in the medial prefrontal cortex and posterior cingulate areas of the brain connected to self-related processing. That, says Cascio, suggests that increases in self-related processing act as a kind of emotional buffer to any painful, negative, or threatening information that follows. Behavior change is often difficult, Cascio explains, because messages that offer advice can be threatening to people's sense of competence and positive self-regard."

Self-affirmation theory suggests that people are motivated to maintain a positive self-view and that threats to perceived self-competence are met with resistance. When threatened, self-affirmations can restore self-competence by allowing individuals to reflect on sources of self-worth, such as core values. When examined, the neural mechanisms of self-affirmation with a task developed for use in FMRI results demonstrated that participants who were affirmed showed increased activity in key regions of the brain's self-processing medial prefrontal cortex, posterior cingulate cortex, and valuation ventral striatum.

Furthermore, this neural activity went on to predict changes in sedentary behavior consistent with successful affirmation in response to a separate physical activity intervention. These results highlight neural processes associated with successful self-affirmation, and further suggest that key pathways may be amplified in conjunction with prospection.

Thanks to neuroscience, we now know that certain neural pathways are increased when we practice self-affirmations, making affirmations an excellent way of breaking old limiting beliefs and building new positive beliefs and mindsets. Words are potent, and when directed inwards through the use of positive self-talk, they can transform our internal state on an intense and profound level. Our mind doesn't know the difference between real and pretend, and because of this, affirmations can program our mind into believing the stated concept. Basically speaking, affirmations help "rewire" the brain. Hence, the use of *Love and Obey* affirmations to reprogram past patriarchal conditioning.

Our subconscious mind has been built over years and years. It's been built on an accumulation of thoughts, memories, beliefs, experiences, and emotions. Change is a process and will not happen overnight, and it takes 72 hours to create a new neural connection. The more we repeat our affirmation and truly feel ourselves into the new experience, the easier it will be to create the connection. Once we've made that connection only then can we build on it and create a more optimistic future. We must allow ourselves the time to be the change we want to be, but, in the meantime, act like we have what it is that we're affirming. It takes repetition to change our affirmation from being a statement to becoming an undeniable belief. "Fake it till you make it" is a well-known phrase, but remember, it takes repetition, repetition, repetition to build the new pattern.

When to Use Affirmations

Affirmations may be used anytime, anyplace, anywhere. However, it's been scientifically proven that the best time to state our affirmations is the last thing at night just as we're about to fall asleep or first thing in the morning as we're waking up. During these times, the brain is in the barely conscious state, known as theta brain waves. This is where our conscious and subconscious worlds meet. While in the theta state, we're withdrawn from the external world and focused on our internal signals. During Theta, our mind is capable of deep and profound learning as we tend to absorb whatever material we're presented with, in a totally accepting and uncritical fashion.

Dr. Bruce Lipton describes the subconscious mind as being similar to a tape recorder. It records our experiences and then plays them back. The more we affirm our new programming, the easier it will be to override the old negative ones. *Love and Obey* affirmations may be used at any time during sex or if you are alone. Nighttime is probably the best time, but you should ensure you are in a relaxed state and have set aside time and a quiet place to do them. Of course, *Love and Obey* affirmations are meant to bring your Queen and you together, so feel free to memorize and recite them during sex, foreplay, or date night.

CHAPTER 5

What are Love and Obey Affirmations?

Love & *Obey* Female Led Affirmations are positive messages that help to reprogram patriarchal thinking and help you and your Queen with the creation of the perfect Female Led Relationship. When applied to your *Love* & *Obey* Female Worship, these affirmations will be instrumental in helping to transform your thinking and your relationship with your Queen. *Love and Obey* affirmations help men to show their devotion to their Queen. It deepens their acceptance of their woman as the supreme leader. These affirmations contain powerful female superiority messages in a crystal-clear audio presentation.

Words are very powerful and research shows that words can affect our brains, how we perceive our world, and affect others. Japanese scientist Masaru Emoto performed experiments on frozen water in the late 1990s and tested the crystallization through the use of positive and negative verbiage. To one group of water, he spoke negative words and phrases, and to the other, he spoke positive words and phrases. After a period of time, the negative group produced ugly, cloudy crystal formations, while the positive group produced clear, beautiful crystals. The point of the study was to demonstrate the power of words and their impact on how living things are transformed. The words that we use in our daily life are a habit. Any statement we read, see, or speak regularly is seen as more valid than one we're exposed to only occasionally. Encouraging affirmations are a powerful way to express love in a relationship. It is a method often neglected by many people.

If both you and your Queen's love language are words of affirmation, you can be certain that any affirmation you give will have a powerful impact on her. For this to be of maximum impact, the words of affirmation you give should be regular. Your Queen will then feel the love you are trying to express. Affirmations can be used to show your appreciation of her. The most powerful appreciations are often for small, almost overlooked things, and they give your Queen an element of surprise and delight.

In fact, that appreciation may even be unexpected and would cause your "words of affirmation" to really change her.

Something more common is our habit of using negative words or phrases over and over again. The more we use and hear words or phrases, the more it becomes normal and the more power it has over us, thus the more it shapes us. Neuroscientists have a name for this automatic habit of the brain, which is called negativity bias. It's an adaptive trait of human psychology. It activates a cascade of stress hormones and leaves us fixated on potential threats.

The Power of Self-Talk

Self-talk is a growing research field, especially as it relates to sports performance. In one study, basketball players instructed to self-talk using the word "relax" experienced enhanced performance results when compared to those who either didn't self-talk at all or used the word "fast." Likewise, a 2017 study found that positive self-talk increased tennis players' "enjoyment and perseverance." What is it about self-talk that helps athletes perform at such high levels? Researchers believe it has to do with attention. Self-talk serves to help people focus, blocking out distractions and minimizing ego. Given this mechanism, you would expect self-talk to influence performance outside of sports, and you'd be right.

Though perception is often thought of as merely a mental process, it isn't all in our heads. There is evidence that language changes the very biology of how we process the world around us. In a 2013 study, that language has a real impact on our systems of perception research, which showed words influenced the ability to see certain shapes over others. Gary Lupyan, a University of Wisconsin-Madison psychology professor, says, "If language affects performance on a test like this, it indicates that language is influencing vision at a pretty early stage. It's getting really deep into the visual system."

This is one reason why affirmations are so powerful and can bring about change. Thoughts are energy, signals created in our minds that travel out into the world. And just like the phone or TV signal that has a "mission" when they go out, so do our thoughts. Our thoughts' mission is to bring back to you exactly what you think about. Now, fortunately, this isn't an immediate response or our world would be in chaos, but a consistent thought repeated over and over again develops power to eventually have those results show up in your life.

In ancient magic, language and words had deep importance in   spells. Unlike in modern day movies, like Harry Potter where they say a variety of strange phrases like *Avada Kedavra*, practitioners of magic in ancient Greek and Rome used spells to "bind" people up to different outcomes. Spells had known formulas and named involved parties, like gods and people, and then connected them to actions or results. You could use a binding spell to invoke an upcoming athletic victory or ensure your happy marriage to a new partner—and to do so, you'd use powerful strings of words passed on by magicians or ordinary people.

Words were considered very powerful and sacred. Just as exercise can change our bodies, so can mental activity, such as learning and using language, shape the physical structures of our brains. When two neurons respond to a stimulus, such as a word, they begin to form chemical and physical pathways to each other, which are strengthened or weakened depending on how often they are co-activated. This process of "neurons that fire together, wire together" is the basis for all learning, and is reflected in the formation of gray matter and white matter.

The brain's ability to adapt to its environment explains how we become specialized to the sounds of our native tongue. All infants are born with the ability to discriminate between the speech sounds of different languages, but eventually become tuned to the inputs they hear the most; neural pathways corresponding to native phonemes are strengthened, while those corresponding to foreign sounds are pruned. For bilinguals, this window of "universal" sound processing stays open longer because of their exposure to richer language environments. In other words, the inputs that our brains receive shape how we experience the world around us.

As we learned, affirmations come out of self-affirmation theory, which suggests that people have a fundamental motivation to maintain self-integrity. By doing it together, you increase your bond and intimacy. Use it to spice up your sex life and spend more time together. As a female empowerment author, I have seen firsthand how female led life has dramatically improved the lives of couples who fully immerse themselves in this lifestyle. *Love and Obey* affirmations serve to support the transition to this life and bring the couple together. Affirmations remind both men and women of the significance of this relationship and deepens particularly your man's understanding of FLR.

A man, by default, craves feminine softness and the kind of closeness and intimacy only a woman can give. Once he's hooked, he's not going anywhere. The problem with most relationships is something that starts so passionate, rapidly begins its downhill slide due to a lack of understanding of what each other needs. Couples who start being so adoring of each other remain in a loveless, sexless relationship in which what they need to do is merely tolerating each other. Female led marriages and FLR is changing all of this.

Today, there are thousands of men who are eager to find and serve a female led woman, but when they must fully submit, as in instances where there is a disagreement, they will often fail and revert to learned and conditioned behavior.

When a man understands that the Queen is always in charge, she is supreme, and he is less likely to act out and is more open to her direction. n female led life, sex is for her pleasure. Men will often revert to past patterns when they are attempting to be sexually satisfied. Sometimes they are unable to fully satisfy a woman the way a Queen needs to be pleasured until they fully submit to her command in all areas. When sex is for the Queen's pleasure, men need to satisfy her orally first, then they are free to focus on their own orgasm. This presents a perfect opportunity to add *Love and Obey* affirmations while he pleasures his Queen. By repeating these affirmations during sex, he deepens his understanding that sex is for her pleasure first, and she is the sole focus.

Why is this important? Often relationships are challenging, and it is only in the day-to-day practices we can encourage good behavior. In theory, proper practice of all of the principles I have outlined in my books *Love and Obey* and *Real Men Worship Women* should help couples to create more happiness and intimacy but only if both men and women accept their new roles and men particularly can release past conditioning. Women are already in the position to take the lead as they are encouraged to lead in other aspects of their lives. Some who are still on the fence may need encouragement, but when a man submits and encourages his Queen to lead, she will naturally take control. Men on the other hand, may need more help because they are trying to overcome years of conditioning.

Repetition and corresponding mental images formed when saying my *Love & Obey* Female Led Affirmations will help you to change your patriarchal conditioning. When repeating my *Love & Obey* Female Led Affirmations over and over again, a man becomes open suggestions of total submission to women. This is beneficial because it only strengthens the relationship for both people to be working toward a common goal.

University College London's Dr. Scott states, "The brain takes speech and separates it into words and "melody"—the varying intonation in speech that reveals mood, gender, and so on. Words are then shunted over to the left temporal lobe for processing while the melody is channeled to the right side of the brain, a region more stimulated by music." This new research is ground-breaking because it explains why the rhythm and intonation of a person's voice affect us on such a deep emotional level. How you repeat your affirmations to yourself and with your Queen can have a profound effect.

Ideally, my *Love & Obey* Female Led Affirmations should be repeated in a quiet space with serious concentration and focus on releasing all prior conditioning. Men have been programmed for centuries by our patriarchal society, and there is the tendency to fall back into old patterns. Even though these affirmations are aimed at being completed when you are intimate with your Queen, the benefits will transfer to daily life. Many common disagreements on decisions will be eliminated, when you have fully decided to commit to serving your Queen properly each day. This also means changes in bad habits like raising your voice, being disrespectful, storming out during a discussion, arguing when given an order, and engaging in excessive masturbation or watching porn without her express consent.

In the movie *The Crown*, I was impressed to see how every member of the Queen household, as well as all visitors, including other members of royalty, government, media, and her children, had to abide by proper etiquette and rules to address the Queen. I was fascinated by how, at no time, was anyone ever able to break those rules nor would they dare. The same is true of your devotion and service to your Queen. To refresh you on the rules, please refer to my book *Real Men Worship Women. Love and Obey* affirmations are essentially your commitment to ensuring that these rules on proper service of your Queen and accepting her as true authority reigns above all else. Nothing comes before your devotion and commitment to your Queen. When you repeat these affirmations, they should be said and believed with this purpose.

Love & Obey Female Led Affirmations should be repeated when your subconscious mind is most receptive: after waking and immediately before going to sleep. Repeat my Erotic Affirmations during sex, either silently or out loud. The goal is to become a master female led life and a pro of worshipping your Queen. Some people find it incredibly powerful to enjoy repeating them during sex. They believe my erotic *Love & Obey* Female Led Affirmations enhance their love, passion, pleasure, exploration, and devotion to their Queen during sex. This deepens the psychological aspect. Satisfaction with sexual relations is one of the important factors in satisfying marital life and the health and quality of life of couples and is one of the most important indicators of life satisfaction. Sexual satisfaction refers to a person's feelings during sex as in how enjoyable it is. Sexual satisfaction is of particular importance in family and marital affairs, and several studies have pointed to the effect of sexual satisfaction on marital satisfaction.

It is estimated that 80 percent of marital conflicts and disagreements are due to the lack of sexual satisfaction between husband and wife. It has also been proven that sexual dissatisfaction is the cause of many psychological disturbances, increasing the rate of betrayal and divorce. Studies show sexual satisfaction as one of the physiological needs of basic human health, and in the absence of it, the physical and psychological stress caused by it will disrupt the individual's health, reduce his abilities and creativity, and risk of strengthening the marital relationship.

Psychological variables are important among the factors affecting marital satisfaction. In this regard, emotional intelligence and spiritual intelligence are psychological variables that affect marital satisfaction or dissatisfaction. Research studies show that there is a positive and significant relationship between emotional intelligence and sexual satisfaction, with increased emotional intelligence and sexual satisfaction. The results of the study of emotional intelligence components showed that only the emotional adjustment component had a significant relationship with sexual satisfaction. According to the research on spouses' relationships, emotional intelligence components seem to be effective in marital satisfaction.

Sincere relationships between couples require communication skills, such as individual attention to issues from the perspective of their spouses and the ability to empathic understanding of what their partner experiences, as well as being sensitive and aware of their needs. In a study by Schutte and Malouff on a sample of spouses, they found that those who scored elevated emotional intelligence scores were significantly more matched with marital satisfaction. *Love and Obey* affirmations improve the emotional part of sex and helps men to tap into this side, which leads to more overall happiness in sex and the relationship.

Patriarchal conditioning is limited because it fails to even address emotional intelligence, which makes it ill-suited for marital happiness and it is probably a significant factor in the rise in divorces. If this is true, then isn't it reasonable to focus on changing and reprogramming this patriarchal conditioning as soon as possible. Hence the reason for my encouragement of the *Love and Obey* movement and using these affirmations. *Love and Obey* affirmations are reminders to your unconscious mind to stay focused on your goals and to come up with solutions to challenges and obstacles that might get in the way. They can also create higher vibrations for happiness, joy, appreciation, and gratitude, that then, through the law of attraction, magnetize people, resources, and opportunities to come your way to help you achieve your goals. You can release yourself from patriarchal conditioning. If you want to be truly happy and live a female led life, you're going to need to let go of insecurities caused by patriarchal conditioning. Using *Love and Obey* affirmations with daily practice is a good step.

Domination and submission are two complementary roles in a Female Led Relationship. The dominant female is the active force in the relationship, controlling their male partner to various limits, which are understood and agreed upon and grow deeper during different evolutionary stages of their relationship. A submissive relinquishes a portion of their control to their dominant for the purposes of sexual and emotional satisfaction. These roles apply outside of the bedroom as well. But for the purposes of my *Love & Obey* Female Led Lifestyle Affirmations, we will only discuss them in their sexual capacity.

Keep in mind that the female is always the dominant, and the male is always the submissive, which means they have swapped roles from the traditional patriarchal relationship. This is what these *Love & Obey* Female Led Affirmations are all about, eliminating all remnants of patriarchal thought from the male mind, so that he has complete acceptance of female superiority. An important part of using *Love and Obey* affirmations is to repeat them with this allegiance in mind. Each time you repeat your affirmations, you are also releasing the control to your Queen. With each word, you are accepting her as your supreme leader and you are committing yourself to serving her.

Communication before you begin is important. Negotiate limits and boundaries. Before every single erotic affirmations session, check on each other. Make sure you are both comfortable. It's probably not a good time if you are both experiencing stress and anxiety. Wait until things calm down, so you can make this a wonderful experience and reprogram together. Since this will be new for you as a man, to surrender more power and control, you should take it step-by-step.

In this case, discussing and repeating the *Love & Obey* Female Led Affirmations together is critical for you and your Queen to be on the same page. Never attempt to force anything. If there are disagreements or hesitation, then you both need to discuss further. Openly talk about what you are both willing and unwilling to do under the influence of my positive Female Led Relationship *Love & Obey* Female Led Affirmations.

Remember, sometimes FLR involves you having to perform undesirable tasks, so you and your Queen need to be allowed to set as many limits as needed.

CHAPTER 6

Your Obedience Affirmations

Session One

Welcome to your first session to begin practicing your affirmations. This practice can be done together with your Queen in a specific, designated time when there are no distractions or when you're both alone. So, turn off your phones, put the kids to bed, and find a quiet space—maybe in the privacy of your bedroom to complete this session. Get comfortable, and it may be easier for you both to follow along. Take a few moments to calm down, check your breathing, and get into a calm, almost meditative state.

Love & Obey Female Led Affirmations should be repeated with intention. The first one can be loud, then you can gradually lower to a whisper. My suggestion is to repeat them four times and really focus on the words and your Queen's voice. While a great deal of sexual attraction may revolve around the visual, evidence suggests sounds are just as important. Voices can communicate a great deal of social and biological information that can either be a turn on or a turnoff, says the researchers led by Susan Hughes, an assistant professor of Psychology at Albright College in Reading, PA. As you talk slower and quieter, subconsciously, you will become more and more relaxed and move to a receptive state.

It is important to start with a deep breath in through your nose and breathe out through your mouth. Repeat this process until you start to feel relaxed. With each deep breath, you should gently bring yourself to a consistent and normal level of breathing. *Love and Obey* affirmations can be used while you are making love. Some couples create a ritual for the affirmations and lovemaking combined whereas others just use it as foreplay. This is a fabulous idea because it reinforces the intentional and sacred aspect of the affirmations and places it in a central place in your lives.

What you are essentially doing is you repeat these affirmations in a very relaxed state. This is not the time for rough, wild sex. The gentle pleasure of your lovemaking will help your subconscious associate the *Love & Obey* Female Led Affirmations with pleasure and intimacy with your partner, so the results will be powerful. If you are doing it in a room alone, which is also very effective, do everything to help relax your mind and focus on your breathing. Repeat the simple *Love & Obey* Female Led Affirmations by becoming quieter and softer spoken each time as the session continues. If you decide to do them together, the Queen will repeat the first line, and you, the man and her supportive gentleman, will say the second bolded line.

Here are the basic steps to follow as you begin your practice of reciting your affirmations.

Step One: Breathe in through your nose, and out through your mouth.

Step Two: Repeat each of the below *Love & Obey* Female Led Affirmations four times; First, loudly, and second, in a normal volume. Third, softly and fourth, silently to yourself.

I am loving to my Queen at all times.

(Repeat 4 Times)

I am obedient to my Queen.

(Repeat 4 Times)

I serve my Queen and attend to her needs as requested.

(Repeat 4 Times)

I belong only to My Queen, and I do not answer to anyone over Her.

(Repeat 4 Times)

I serve my Queen's desires first above my own.

(Repeat 4 Times)

I attend to my Queen's pleasure first before my own.

(Repeat 4 Times)

My work is for my Queen, at work and at home.

(Repeat 4 Times)

I submit to my Queen's power.

(Repeat 4 Times)

I find peace through connecting to my Queen's Divine.

(Repeat 4 Times)

I submit with my whole being to my Queen's command.

(Repeat 4 Times)

My Queen's joy and happiness each day is my mission.

(Repeat 4 Times)

I obey my Queen's demands without question or argument.

(Repeat 4 Times)

It is important that you focus on repeating the lines while becoming aware of your breathing. This creates a meditative state, which prepares the mind for acceptance of this new conditioning. If you choose to do your affirmations during sex, then keep it slow and intentional. Practice with a few lines at first so you get into the rhythm. Your Queen should also be comfortable as she repeats her lines. The most important part of this process is to do your affirmations regularly and with intention.

Visualization and Affirmations

Visualization is great to add to your affirmations. Visualization techniques have been used by successful people to help them to achieve their desired outcomes for decades. The daily practice of visualizing your dreams as already complete can rapidly accelerate your achievement of those dreams, goals, and ambitions. With affirmations, you are visualizing what you are repeating. If you repeat that you accept the Queen as supreme, you are visualizing you both engaging happily together, and you are allowing her to be in control.

There are a few benefits to adding visualization: One, including it activates your creative subconscious which will start generating creative ideas to achieve your goal. Two, it programs your brain to more readily perceive and recognize the resources you will need to achieve your dreams. Three, it activates the universal creative force, thereby drawing to you what you want. In this case, pictures of you fully submitting to your woman. Images of both of you happy and fulfilled having the best sex of your life. Visualization builds the internal motivation and it is a powerful, transformation combination of affirmations and visualization.

Obedience is the cornerstone of a Female Led Relationship. It is the act of following orders without question because they come from an authority that you have accepted. There are many legitimate authorities in a person's life, from parents to teachers to law enforcement, and even spiritual and government leaders. Most of these authority figures mentioned above were given their authority by society. We are just told to follow what they tell us to do. In other words, we are trained to be obedient to these people. At some time in their life, every person has followed a superior without questioning why they are doing what they are doing.

For example, we never question why we take tests in school. We just take them because we are told to do so. We never question a lot of the rules that people say "are in our best interest" because they are usually told to us by someone in a position higher. In the Female Led Relationship, the woman is granted the highest position of authority, and the man agrees to obey her. In exchange, he earns the right to live in a safe, loving, and compassionate female led lifestyle.

Chaos is a situation of confusion, a disorderly state, and lacking leadership. With an accepted authority figure and strict obedience, any guesswork on what to do goes away, and reduces anxiety on how to respond in various situations. Loving female authority gives her control over you and also expects your obedience. Her orders and your obedience determine the positions of power that define the role of you and your woman. Once you accept your woman as your

Queen, and she accepts you as her obedient gentleman, you will see that you have eliminated elements of a presumption and incidents of confusion.

CHAPTER 7

Your Sexual Worship Affirmations

S exual Worship Affirmations can be done just lying together or during your sexual session. It can help to get you both relaxed and heightens the mood.

Use it as foreplay or during intercourse for an even more intense experience. As you repeat the lines, think deeply and focus on the pleasure you are giving to your Queen. You are attempting to excite every part of her body. Focus on the sensations, sounds, rhythms, and how she feels. Let her voice fill your entire being. Some couples choose to use these as foreplay together with roleplay and to increase the excitement. Use it in a ritual as you prepare to worship your Goddess. Add some sexy massage to heighten the physical touch experience.

Many couples enjoy adding a spiritual element in which sex is viewed as sacred and sexuality is seen as a positive expression of the life force. This perspective was the norm in many cultures pre-dating Greek and Roman times and these societies date back 30,000 years. Even as late as 3,500 years ago, those who lived on the island of Crete recognized sexual pleasure as a wonderful way to connect with spirit, renew the abundance of the land, and unite deeply with one another. In this culture, sexuality was widely understood as a pathway to spiritual ecstasy.

The fact is that sexuality and spirituality were never split until well into the first millennium of the Common Era when denial of the body became the popular theology of the day. It may seem outrageous to view sexuality in such lofty terms. Yet, it no longer makes sense to deny the spiritual dimension of our sexuality. Author Thomas Merton said, "Uninhibited erotic love between married persons, properly understood, sexual union is an expression of deep personal love and a means to the deepening, perfecting, and sanctifying of that love." When pure, sexual love can take on a sacred quality. Spiritual development involving mastery of sexual energy, in the context of trusting and spiritually mature, male-female relationships, reveal the possibility of a fruitful merging of sex and spirituality. Affirmations can be used to deepen the sexual experience and merge the spiritual. Loving and feeling loved, you will feel more content, less driven, at peace within, more spontaneous, as well as joyful.

Since sexual energy is the source of our connection to the life force, the benefits to physical, emotional, and mental health are obvious. Developing conscious rituals and techniques allow you to become more open to such transcendent experiences. It prepares you to be receptive to the possibility of connecting in higher states of awareness from peak sexual moments.

Here is an easy way to begin using your affirmations during sex. Start at your Queen's feet, ankles, shins, knees, thighs, hips, vagina, stomach, breasts, arms, and enjoy it very slowly. Stop at each body part and repeat a full chant four times before moving to the next body part. Go slowly and gently. Take as much time as possible on each body part, and if you want, repeat multiple chants four times on each body part. You and your Queen should be in a very relaxed, open, and in receptive state of mind throughout the entire session. Focus your attention even more intensely on each affirmation. When you are thinking about each affirmation, imagine how you can involve your five senses in the experience. You may use them as foreplay or a short ritual before your lovemaking session. You may also add them during your intercourse or at the end of your session. When you are starting, it is probably best to focus on them in the beginning of your lovemaking. Begin by you both getting into a very comfortable position.

I accept my place at the feet of my Queen by loving and massaging her feet.

(Repeat 4 Times)

I serve my Queen's body with all of my energy.

(Repeat 4 Times)

I am ready and willing to do anything sexually that my Queen requests.

(Repeat 4 Times)

I place my entire trust with my Queen.

(Repeat 4 Times)

My Queen's sexual pleasure comes first.

(Repeat 4 Times)

I take care of Her sexual needs, and she takes care of mine.

(Repeat 4 Times)

I focus on my Queen's sexual needs and aim to be the best at fulfilling them.

(Repeat 4 Times)

I am owned by my Queen.

(Repeat 4 Times)

My purpose is loyal and proper service to my Queen.

(Repeat 4 Times)

My daily goal is to make my Queen happy.

(Repeat 4 Times)

My Queen's orgasm is more important than my own orgasm.

(Repeat 4 Times)

Sex is only for the Queen's pleasure above mine.

(Repeat 4 Times)

I ensure my Queen is sexually satisfied during each session.

(Repeat 4 Times)

She is my one and only Queen.

(Repeat 4 Times)

I am 100% obedient to my Queen.

(Repeat 4 Times)

During Oral Sex

As you know in Female Led Relationships, sex is for her pleasure and nothing is more important than satisfying her needs first. The following affirmations can be used as you pleasure your Queen. Focus deeply on connecting to her divine as you repeat them.

I submit to loving and exploring every inch of my Queen's vagina.

(Repeat 4 Times)

My Queen's orgasm comes first

(Repeat 4 Times)

I enjoy the taste, smell, and feel of my Queen's vagina.

(Repeat 4 Times)

I am becoming a pro at satisfying my Queen orally.

(Repeat 4 Times)

My Queen's oral pleasure comes first.

(Repeat 4 Times)

I will begin every sexual session connecting to my Queen's divine through oral pleasure.

(Repeat 4 Times)

Penis Submission Affirmations

My penis responds only to my Queen's command

(Repeat 4 Times)

My penis shows my devotion to my Queen.

(Repeat 4 Times)

My penis grows rock hard and thick only for my Queen.

(Repeat 4 Times)

I remain hard and ready to serve my Queen.

(Repeat 4 Times)

My penis is owned by my Queen.

(Repeat 4 Times)

I lust only to serve and obey my Queen.

(Repeat 4 Times)

My penis exists only to serve my Queen as much as she desires.

(Repeat 4 Times)

Tantric Sex

Adding affirmations to Tantric sex is perfect because you are already going to be in a meditative state for both. The three major keys to moving energy in tantra are breath, sound, and movement. Using these three keys, you can practice "running" your sexual energy throughout your body, whether you're engaged in sensual play or alone, and you can amp it up until it spills over into energetic orgasm. It can be such a profound and empowering aspect of connecting with your own innate sensuality. Steps to begin to get into the Tantric sex mood include getting prepared and creating the kind of space you'd like to be in to have any other kind of orgasm.

Foreplay can be anything you want it to be—oral, a massage, taking a shower together. But whatever you do, make sure you and your partner are fully present. Sit in front of your man. Look into each other's eyes. Start to move your bodies slightly as you breathe. After five minutes, start to touch each other sensually, taking turns massaging each other's arms, legs, neck, and other parts. After another five minutes, begin to kiss—and only kiss. Focus on every physical sensation you're feeling in the moment.

You both need to go within. Turn your attention inward, closing the eyes to signal to the mind that it's time to relax and let go. Open up the breath. Take some long, deep breaths to start, relaxing your entire body. Let the breath melt through any tension anywhere inside you. Then move into circular breathing, with no pause between the exhales or inhales. Connect to your sensuality. Focus your attention at the level of the genitals; connect to the quality of pleasure and eroticism within you. Fantasizing and caressing the whole body can help get you in the mood. Massage is vital to Tantric sex. You may perform your affirmations at any point before or during your session. Mix it up to keep your sex fresh and exciting.

Tantric sex involves sexual energy that goes beyond physical sensations of pleasure and genital orgasms. It is not limited to genital stimulation and the release of tension through a quick and simple orgasm. When spiritual sex is consciously practiced, there is a quality of "mindfulness," which is heightened awareness and expanded consciousness. The more cosmic experiences utilizing sexual energy create ecstatic states. The essence of tantric sex is enhanced awareness, extraordinary inspiration, and a sense of merging with the life force.

What Tantric and spiritual experience of sex can do is increase conscious loving, which is sexual energy that generates intense, loving feelings for the partner. The result is greater partner connection, reinforcing commitment in a long-term relationship through loving communion, enhancing the bond. The second level is spiritual union which is the ultimate expression of sexuality. Often one receives inspiration and illumination that can be translated into divine guidance or simply experienced as pure bliss. These transcendental sexual experiences produce a sense of merging with the source of energy and losing physical boundaries during orgasm. It is often described as "being in the moment of boundless bliss." Many ancient and modern visionary experiences are described as feelings of being "bathed in pure light." It is cosmic orgasm, the direct experience of the self as pure energy, in union with a divine source. This level of spiritual sex may occur without a partner and even without any physical stimulation.

Post-Session Communication

After any kind of sexual *Love and Obey* Female Led Affirmation session, may require you to calm yourself or your partner down. Your Affirmations may simply become too powerful, and you may have to lower the excitement from your minds. Make sure you schedule enough time in your session for a calming down period. The need to be physically and emotionally comforted is perfectly normal after an intense *Love & Obey* Female Led Affirmation journey. It is important you have comfortable items around you, such as bedding, favorite food, and even some beverages close at hand should you both want them. This is something important for you both to enjoy and require from each other. You have a responsibility to comfort your Queen after an intense sexual *Love & Obey* Female Led Affirmation experience.

Be sure to set aside some time for open communication on how the session went. Discuss everything. What was good, and what did not work. This helps to perform a check that you are both enjoying the session and that it was effective. Note anything you may want to change at your next session.

How to Improve Communication:

1. **Learn to be calm and relaxed.** If a conversation is making you angry, anxious, or frustrated, learning to self-soothe is key. If you respond from an angry place, or if you are anxious, nervous, or scared, you are likely to say things you don't mean, words that are hurtful, point blame, and/or criticize. Practice breathing. Take long deep breaths and count to ten. Go outside for some fresh air. It's okay to say, "I will be right back, I need a break." Practice breathing often, not just during a heated conversation, but while driving, while at your desk, even while relaxing. Breathing is at the core of becoming calm. And the absolute best time to talk is when you are calm.

2. **Be nonjudgmental.** Shut your critical and emotional mind off and really listen to what your partner is saying. Empathize by putting yourself in your partner shoes, if you need to.

3. **Use positive language.** This is also about remembering to avoid blaming, pointing the finger, criticizing, and judging. Instead, say things about your

feelings. For example, instead of saying, "You don't even try to please me," try this: "I really feel unsatisfied with our lovemaking these days." Focus on using "I feel" and avoid using "you" in the sentence.

4. **Listen.** Summarize, paraphrase, or repeat what your partner has said. This is an easy way to let your partner know you have heard them and can (often) diffuse an angry situation. If your partner says, "I am angry and sexually frustrated these days, and you don't seem to care about sex," instead of responding defensively, which might be your inkling, this is a great opportunity for you to make the conversation productive. You can respond by saying, "It sounds like you are feeling dissatisfied with our sex life. Perhaps we could find a solution."

5. **Touch while talking.** Holding your partner's hand or putting your hand on his/her knee can remind you and your partner that you are on his/her side, and that you two are in this together. It promotes intimacy

6. **Compliment.** Compliments are a big part of positive talk. It's important for our partners to feel recognized and appreciated. I recommend a minimum of three compliments a day. The best way to catch a bee is with sugar.

How do we improve trust in communication? Effective communication is based on trust, and if we don't trust the person speaking, we're not going to listen to their words. Trust begins with eye contact because we need to see the person's face to evaluate if they are being deceitful or not. Gentle eye contact increases trustworthiness and encourages future cooperation and a happy gaze will increase emotional trust.

However, if we see the slightest bit of anger or fear on the speaker's face, our trust will rapidly decrease. But you can't fake trustworthiness because the muscles around your mouth and eyes that reflect contentment and sincerity are involuntary. The tone of your voice is equally important when it comes to understanding what a person is really trying to say. If the facial expression expresses one emotion, but if the tone conveys a different one, neural dissonance takes place in the brain, causing the person confusion.

Therefore, it is extremely important that you and your Queen look each other in the eye when you are both reciting affirmations. This serves to make the experience so much more powerful and will establish an intimate trust bond between you. In Compassionate Communication, we ask participants to speak only one sentence at a time, slowly, and then listen deeply as the other person speaks for ten seconds or less. This exercise will increase your overall consciousness about the importance of effective communication.

CHAPTER 8

Your Service Affirmations

These are the *Love & Obey* Female Led Affirmations specifically designed for you as a supportive gentleman. As you are aware, service is an extremely important part of Female Led Relationships. Some of your daily service tasks will be as follows:

1. Rub her feet with lotion.

2. Offer to run a bath for her.

3. Assist her around the house and start doing the laundry, clean the kitchen and bathroom, and wash the dishes.

4. Bring her a cup of coffee and breakfast in bed on the weekend.

5. Give her a full body massage.

6. Let her watch what she wants on TV, or let her choose which movie to go see or which restaurant she wants to dine in on Friday night.

7. In general, ask her if there is anything you can do for her. Always act like a gentleman: open her car door, pull out her chair in the restaurant, give her your coat when it's cold out, etc.

8. Do the grocery and shopping.

9. Complete any other tasks she requires around the house.

Your *Love and Obey* service affirmations require you to focus on being the perfect supportive gentleman and your service to the Queen.

I crave my Queen's control over me.
(Repeat 4 Times)

My Queen is in charge. I release my power to her.
(Repeat 4 Times)

I love and accept my submissive nature, just as my Queen loves and accepts my submissive nature.
(Repeat 4 Times)

I constantly look for new ways to serve my Queen.
(Repeat 4 Times)

I am constantly discovering new ways to improve my obedience and submission to my Queen.
(Repeat 4 Times)

My life is more exciting because my Queen rules over it.
(Repeat 4 Times)

I am my happiest when serving my Queen.
(Repeat 4 Times)

I live in the paradise that is my Queen's eyes.
(Repeat 4 Times)

When my Queen speaks, I listen.

(Repeat 4 Times)

I take care of myself, so I may be able to take proper care of my Queen.

(Repeat 4 Times)

I go above and beyond for my Queen every day.

(Repeat 4 Times)

I live to see Her spoiled. I love to see all Her needs met.

(Repeat 4 Times)

She is the only Queen I want. She is the only Queen I need.

(Repeat 4 Times)

It is my duty and privilege to provide for my Queen.

(Repeat 4 Times)

I trust my Queen completely.

(Repeat 4 Times)

My Queen's goals, dreams, and aspirations are important to me.

(Repeat 4 Times)

My life purpose and primary focus is to please my Queen.

(Repeat 4 Times)

I am proud to be owned by my powerful Queen.

(Repeat 4 Times)

I greet my Queen properly each day.

(Repeat 4 Times)

I submit to serving all of my Queen's requests.

(Repeat 4 Times)

I am seeking new ways to serve and submit to my Queen.

(Repeat 4 Times)

My Queen is in charge. I have given all my power to Her.

(Repeat 4 Times)

I am happiest when I am giving to my Queen.

(Repeat 4 Times)

I focus on improving my service to my Queen every day.

(Repeat 4 Times)

CHAPTER 9

Your Submission Affirmations

Researchers believe that interest in submitting to loving female authority begins in childhood. Sigmund Freud's psychoanalytic theory called the Oedipus complex suggests that children have sexual desires for their opposite-sex parent while viewing their same-sex parent as a rival. Some men desire a dominant "mother figure," and 83 percent of single parent households are headed up by the mother. Currently, one in four kids under the age of 18 are raised without a father, or about 16.4 million children. So, a significant number of people are raised in single parent homes where the mother is dominant.

According to Freud's theory, men will have the desire for their mothers who generally now have to be strong independent women who will do the disciplining, hence their desire for discipline from a strong woman in a Female Led Relationship. Women from Freud's theory of identification will want to be like their mothers, therefore, they will naturally take charge, be assertive, and probably want to do the disciplining. Merge these two and you get a very strong sexual desire for men to seek out strong women in a Female Led Relationship.

Why do men want to submit to a strong female in a Female Led Relationship? Below are the following reasons:

1. Men welcome less stress in having to run the household and relationship after taking leadership in work life. This release from authority allows them to relax more with their Queen.

2. Unlike previous generations, men now understand and appreciate the worth of a strong, supportive, and capable woman. They are more willing to encourage their women partners and place them on a pedestal to be treated like a Queen.

3. Men are gravitating to fewer demanding roles in management and senior leadership in corporations, and many are exploring working from home and participating in raising children.

4. Quite simply, fewer arguments and tension. There is less of a power struggle when there are clear distinctions.

Your submission affirmations are the way you allow yourself to completely submit and commit to your Queen. You may use these at any time, and you are encouraged to do them together with your Queen during quiet times, meditation, or during sex. Your Queen will repeat the first lines, and you will repeat your affirmations focusing on the sound of her voice as your ultimate leader and commander. In the submission affirmations, this is your time to allow yourself to release your patriarchal conditioning, forget all that you have previously felt in your relationship, and focus on committing all of your energy to serve your Queen and accepting her as your leader. At this time, you also make the firm decision to place her needs above all others.

Today, men are exploring submission, particularly in a Female Led Relationship, and the one thing that they all discover above anything else is the fact that male submission brings harmony to a home. There is no longer a power struggle between two people who both want to be "in charge." It is a confession of our dependence on one another and an acceptance of our natural roles, the Woman as the leader, the Queen, and the man as her obedient and loyal subject. Do you submit to your boss? If you are given instructions, do you follow them? If you don't, you would face discipline, wouldn't you?! Your Queen is simply the "boss."

I submit to my Queen's leadership.

(Repeat 4 Times)

I will obey my Queen's orders and take her direction.

(Repeat 4 Times)

I heed and listen intently to my Queen's words while she is addressing me.

(Repeat 4 Times)

Submission is my life's purpose and my devotion to my Queen.

(Repeat 4 Times)

My deepest desire is to submit completely to my Queen.

(Repeat 4 Times)

I release a sense of control and submit to my Queen's leadership.

(Repeat 4 Times)

I am becoming more submissive each day.

(Repeat 4 Times)

My Queen leads, and I follow.

(Repeat 4 Times)

I welcome my Queen's loving authority over me.

(Repeat 4 Times)

I refrain from arguing with my Queen.

(Repeat 4 Times)

My Queen makes the decisions for our life, and I accept her direction.

(Repeat 4 Times)

I give myself freely to my Queen.

(Repeat 4 Times)

I accept my Queen's power over me.

(Repeat 4 Times)

I find value in all comments and criticisms and accept them as constructive.

(Repeat 4 Times)

I communicate and discuss my concerns in a very respectful way at all times.

(Repeat 4 Times)

When I hear the sound of my Queen's voice, I listen only.

(Repeat 4 Times)

My Queen controls my heart, mind, and soul.

(Repeat 4 Times)

I am my Queen's submissive, and I belong to my Queen.

(Repeat 4 Times)

My life's purpose is to submit to my Queen, and I was born to serve my Queen.

(Repeat 4 Times)

I submit to my Queen's loving female authority over me.

(Repeat 4 Times)

My mind, heart, and body feel compelled to obey my Queen.

(Repeat 4 Times)

The sight of my Queen and Her voice carry authority and makes me feel compelled to obey.

(Repeat 4 Times)

I will not challenge the words of my Queen. I obediently give myself completely to Her.

(Repeat 4 Times)

When I kneel before my Queen, I experience an intense feeling of submission.

(Repeat 4 Times)

When I kneel before my Queen, I feel like Her slave, and I feel like She rules over me.

(Repeat 4 Times)

I was born to kneel before my Queen. Kneeling feels natural.

(Repeat 4 Times)

Nothing in the world feels better than kneeling before my Queen.

(Repeat 4 Times)

When I kneel, my body feels an intense need to submit to my Queen.

(Repeat 4 Times)

I embrace my feeling of submission, and I allow it to flow through my veins.

(Repeat 4 Times)

Every part of my body desires to submit to my Queen's will.

(Repeat 4 Times)

CHAPTER **10**

Affirmations for Being the Supportive Gentleman

I n a Female Led Relationship, you are the supportive gentleman. It's a crucial role, but affirmations will help you to accept your position and follow the lead of your Queen. There will be things expected of you, so as a reminder, here are the rules of worship:

Your Queen makes the rules, and you must obey them always. No exceptions.

Your Queen creates a list of rules, chores, and regulations for you to follow. They should be reviewed regularly together. This helps to set the expectations and parameters of the relationship.

Establish yourself as a masculine "Knight" figure. She will be your Queen and you are her Knight, which means your purpose in life is to support her and be at her side. You should address her as "Queen" and "Goddess" as much as possible.

Be respectful of her wishes and desires at all times, even when you disagree. Allow your Queen to express her views and listen to her intently.

Keep up with your chores without the need for constant reminders. If she decides that your duties are taking out the garbage and doing the dishes, do them each day without having to be reminded. Your goal is to reduce her responsibility with the domestic chores.

Be attractive to your woman as much as possible. If she likes a beard, grow one. If she enjoys seeing you clean-shaven and in good shape, then do what you can to keep her attraction toward you as much as possible. Staying attractive and practicing good hygiene are key.

Engage in discussions about what ultimately turns her on. Open communication about how to pleasure her is extremely important, and it can make or break a relationship.

Flattery will get you everywhere. Compliment your Queen whenever possible. Your role is to lift her up and help her to be her best each and every day.

Allow your Queen to control the finances if she desires so. Many strong women have managed many aspects of their lives, and they are much better at controlling spending and savings. If the Queen delegates the finances because you are a pro, then that would be the only time it is permissible.

Your Queen controls social activities. Your Queen will decide on a schedule of what is appropriate. This includes what times you both will be home, and when dinner will be ready, etc. If you want to go out, you must ask for the Queen's permission. The enchantresses, magical women in the legends of King Arthur brought balance to a society ruled by male domination. Through their seductive, female magic, they magnetized the men of Camelot. The King's warriors set aside their brutish behavior and broke their backs to court these women. They acted with chivalry in the hopes of earning feminine admiration and tender, female affection. The desire of men to be chivalrous is why these women were able to inspire these men. In modern-day relationships, fighters are you, the men, and you can still honor the laws of chivalry in your Female Led Relationship by becoming your Queen's supportive gentleman and creating more intimacy.

As the supportive gentleman, affirmations help to reinforce your role as to become your Queen's submissive, but strongest supporter. It is important to be comfortable and eager to show your devotion each and every day.

Here are your affirmations to become a better supportive partner.

I am my Queen's biggest champion and supporter.
(Repeat 4 Times)

I am my Queen's Knight in Shining Armor.
(Repeat 4 Times)

My Queen is my focus, even in public.
(Repeat 4 Times)

I am empathetic to my Queen's feelings at all times.
(Repeat 4 Times)

I attend to my Queen's requests over everything.
(Repeat 4 Times)

I address my Queen as "My Queen" whenever I greet her.
(Repeat 4 Times)

My Queen's daily happiness is my life's purpose.

(Repeat 4 Times)

When my Queen is speaking, I refrain from speaking.

(Repeat 4 Times)

My Queen has the last say. She makes the decisions, and I follow her lead.

(Repeat 4 Times)

CHAPTER 11

Your Daily Affirmations

Daily affirmations are the ones you say to yourself when you are going about your daily life. These affirmations will help to remind you daily of your place as the Queen's gentleman and your daily purpose. In a Female Led Relationship, part of your day is devoted to speaking, serving, and treating your Queen respectfully. You will submit to her leadership without question.

Every waking moment I worship my Queen.

(Repeat 4 Times)

I will do as my Queen commands without question.

(Repeat 4 Times)

I will complete the Queen's request immediately as she gives her command.

(Repeat 4 Times)

I listen intently to my Queen's words at all times that we are together.

(Repeat 4 Times)

I attend to my Queen's needs as a supportive gentleman.

(Repeat 4 Times)

I welcome all requests no matter how challenging or time-consuming it is at my Queen's desire.

(Repeat 4 Times)

My Queen's daily leadership makes me a stronger, more disciplined man.

(Repeat 4 Times)

I surrender completely to my Queen leadership.

(Repeat 4 Times)

My goal each day is to improve my level of service to my Queen.

(Repeat 4 Times)

I am proud to be in complete service to my Queen.

(Repeat 4 Times)

I enjoy doing the work that my Queen requests of me.

(Repeat 4 Times)

I answer "Yes, My Queen" to all of her requests.

(Repeat 4 Times)

My goal is to ensure my Queen is happy and content each day.

(Repeat 4 Times)

I am patient and respectful with my Queen.

(Repeat 4 Times)

My Queen is deeply in love with me.

(Repeat 4 Times)

My Queen thinks about me all the time.

(Repeat 4 Times)

My Queen is only attracted to me.

(Repeat 4 Times)

We have a joyous relationship.

(Repeat 4 Times)

I am on the top of her priority list.

(Repeat 4 Times)

My Queen is very affectionate and loving toward me.

(Repeat 4 Times)

My Queen is very caring toward me.

(Repeat 4 Times)

My Queen always treats me with utmost respect.

(Repeat 4 Times)

My Queen worships the ground I walk upon.

(Repeat 4 Times)

My Queen is obsessed with me.

(Repeat 4 Times)

She feels lucky to have me in their life.

(Repeat 4 Times)

We both have a happy and fulfilling relationship.

(Repeat 4 Times)

Our relationship is growing stronger and stronger each day.

(Repeat 4 Times)

My Queen and I communicate with each other in a loving way.

(Repeat 4 Times)

My Queen and I both appreciate and respect each other deeply.

(Repeat 4 Times)

She cherishes me, and she adores me.

(Repeat 4 Times)

My Queen wants to spend Her entire life with me.

(Repeat 4 Times)

I feel comfortable to fully be myself around my Queen.

(Repeat 4 Times)

My Queen feels grateful to have me in her life.

(Repeat 4 Times)

My Queen only has eyes for me.

(Repeat 4 Times)

My Queen finds me magnetic.

(Repeat 4 Times)

My Queen is incredibly supportive of me.

(Repeat 4 Times)

The love between my Queen and I grows stronger and stronger with each day.

(Repeat 4 Times)

No one understands my Queen better than I do.

(Repeat 4 Times)

My relationship with my Queen is loving and harmonious.

(Repeat 4 Times)

My Queen loves me unconditionally.

(Repeat 4 Times)

My Queen and I are excited to talk to each other every single day.

(Repeat 4 Times)

Our bonding is growing stronger and stronger every second.

(Repeat 4 Times)

My Queen and I feel comfortable around each other.

(Repeat 4 Times)

My Queen thinks highly of me.

(Repeat 4 Times)

My Queen and I both give our relationship all the attention we deserve.

(Repeat 4 Times)

I have a beautiful relationship with my Queen.

(Repeat 4 Times)

Our relationship is fulfilling.

(Repeat 4 Times)

My Queen is always trying to make me happy.

(Repeat 4 Times)

CHAPTER **12**

Affirmations to Change Patriarchal Conditioning

P atriarchy means "rule of the father" from ancient Greek. Allen Johnson, a researcher, said "A society is patriarchal to the degree that it is male-dominated, male-identified, and male-centered. The reality of male dominance is clearly seen in the fact that positions of authority are generally held by men or even reserved for men only. Patriarchal societies are male-identified in that the core cultural ideas about what is good, desirable, preferable, or normal are associated with how we think about men and masculinity."

We learn that patriarchy is generally not an explicit ongoing effort by men to dominate women. It is a long-standing system that we are born into and participate in, mostly unconsciously. While most people in a patriarchal hierarchy accept their place in the pecking order, those that do not are generally dealt with by ridicule, coercion, and even violence where necessary. Men often deny the existence, or at least the power of patriarchy, because they do not feel a sense of freedom and a sense of real powerfulness within the system. The truth is that it constricts and restrains everyone, not just the people at the very bottom of its hierarchy.

Now that we have defined the contemporary manifestation of this ancient way of being, and maybe understand how it has managed to perpetuate itself through a couple hundred generations of parents to children, how then do we address challenging and working toward ending this? *Love and Obey* breaks the "gender barrier" by turning everything around. Males submit to females. You will want to focus on releasing your patriarchal conditioning. The whole point of the affirmations is to reprogram your mind to complete acceptance of your Queen as supreme. Releasing old patriarchal conditioning. If you really do want to change, improve your relationships and learn how to make a relationship last, then it is up to you. You can eventually develop and maintain healthy positive relationships.

These affirmations will help you to develop a healthy relationship with your Queen. Mentally dissolve any fears of submitting to her and become more in tune with your partner to bring the right elements of a healthy relationship that are needed. Allow yourself to open up more, discuss your feelings, and develop a relationship built on trust and honesty. Change your mindset and thought patterns for the better, which will change your behavior and lead to a deeper connection. Last, they will reprogram your mind to learn how to move past insecurities that are holding you back.

The ultimate goal is for you and your Queen to have a healthy relationship. This occurs when two people have mutual respect for one another and are able to truly be themselves and simultaneously respect their partner for who they are. This almost always requires compromise, respect, and patience. But the effort is well worth it because, as human beings, we are meant to connect on a deep level with someone we love and know that we are secure in our most important relationship. These affirmations will help you achieve the deep, connected, long-lasting relationship you desire once you are able to reprogram past conditioning and release it. Let it go and submit to your Queen.

My Queen is in control at all times.
(Repeat 4 Times)

I completely accept and follow my Queen's leadership.

(Repeat 4 Times)

I welcome and submit to my Queen's power over me.
(Repeat 4 Times)

I am completely submissive to my Queen who I accept as my supreme ruler.
(Repeat 4 Times)

I trust my Queen completely.
(Repeat 4 Times)

I release my past, patriarchal conditioning and accept my Queen to be in charge.
(Repeat 4 Times)

CHAPTER **13**

Your Queen's Affirmation Training

Now, it's time for you to respond to your Queen's commands. Research shows that your Queen's voice can have a powerful effect on you and this gives you both an opportunity to work on affirmations together and explore how responding to her can help to accelerate your conditioning.

Voice and Effects on Men

Voice is one of the most important social communication cues. Brain regions that respond more strongly to the mother's voice extend beyond auditory areas to include those involved in emotion and reward processing, social functions, detection of what is personally relevant, and face recognition. Vinod Menon, PhD, professor of psychiatry and behavioral sciences, said the children's brains were scanned via magnetic resonance imaging while they listened to short clips of the nonsense-word recordings, some produced by their own mother. The areas of the brain affected were auditory regions, such as the primary auditory cortex; regions of the brain that handle emotions, such as the amygdala and brain regions that detect and assign value to rewarding stimuli, such as the mesolimbic reward pathway and medial prefrontal cortex; regions that process information about the self, including the default mode network; and areas involved in perceiving and processing the sight of faces. "We know that hearing their mother's voice can be an important source of emotional comfort to children," Menon added. "Here, we're showing the biological circuitry underlying that."

Since the Queen essentially becomes a central figure in a man's life, it is possible that the Queen's voice can have a similar effect on men. Scientists at the University of Sheffield have explained the differences in the way the male brain interprets female and male voices. Scientists studied brain scans of twelve male subjects while they listened to male and female voices. It found startling differences in the way that the brain interprets the two sounds, with female voices causing activity in the auditory section of the brain and the male voice sparking activity in the "mind's eye" at the back of the brain. When a man hears a female voice, the auditory section of his brain is activated, which analyses the different sounds in order to "read" the voice and determine the auditory face.

In addition, researchers have discovered that hormonal changes during times of peak fertility in a woman's menstrual cycle may exert a physiological effect on her vocal cords, which may in turn elicit an unconscious response from both male listeners. A new study from James Madison university researchers revealed that when testing the electrical activity in the subjects' skin while they were listening to the recordings of women, electrical activity in the skin increased by roughly 20 percent, and heart rates increased by roughly five percent showing that men were affected, even aroused, by the sound of the female voice. So, based on these studies, it is possible to conclude that when you are able to repeat your *Love and Obey* affirmations together with the Queen, focusing and responding to her voice should make the experience even more powerful and transformative.

Love and Obey women know how to control their men and your Queen can enjoy repeating these affirmations as you show your devotion to her with your responses. These affirmations can also be done while you are sexually worshipping your Queen or the two of you are enjoying some close intimate time. If you are sexually pleasuring her, you will simply stop and repeat "Yes, My Queen" then resume. The goal is for both of you to be excited, engaged, and aroused.

Queen: You will submit to my loving authority. Is that what you want as well?
You: (Repeat "Yes, my Queen.")

Queen: You are completely obedient to me.
You: (Repeat "Yes, my Queen.")

Queen: You serve my every command you.
You: (Repeat "Yes, my Queen.")

Queen: You belong to me, I own you.
You: (Repeat "Yes, my Queen.")

Queen: Your purpose is to ensure my happiness daily.
You: (Repeat "Yes, my Queen.")

Queen: You submit to my command above all others.
You: (Repeat "Yes, my Queen.")

Queen: You will find peace through loyal service to me.

You: (Repeat "Yes, my Queen.")

Queen: My pleasure comes first.

You: (Repeat "Yes, my Queen.")

Queen: You are my one true love and supporter.

You: (Repeat "Yes, my Queen.")

Queen: You love worshipping my pussy, and you are eager to satisfy me.

You: (Repeat "Yes, my Queen.")

Queen: My vagina brings you ultimate pleasure.

You: (Repeat "Yes, my Queen.")

Queen – You are eager to become an oral sex pro to give me the most mind-blowing intense oral session of my life.

You: (Repeat "Yes, my Queen.")

Queen: You accept me as your supreme leader.
You: (Repeat "Yes, my Queen.")

Queen: You surrender completely to me.
You: (Repeat "Yes, my Queen.")

Queen: You will do everything to ensure I am fully sexually satisfied before your own orgasms.
You: (Repeat "Yes, my Queen.")

Queen: You only orgasm with my permission.
You: (Repeat "Yes, my Queen.")

Queen: You only masturbate with my permission.
You: (Repeat "Yes, my Queen.")

CHAPTER **14**

General Affirmations to Be More Centered

O ne of the most important parts of real change is to feel more centered and at peace. Self-esteem can be a crucial peace to allowing this to be your reality. Self-esteem issues can affect your relationship, so it is important to address while going through the use of affirmations. A large part of changing past conditioning is to determine if there are issues with self-esteem, which also holds you back. Ask yourself these questions: Do you have a low self-opinion? Are you constantly comparing yourself to other people, trying to prove yourself to them, but often find yourself feeling inferior to them? Is your lack of self-esteem and self-worth limiting your enjoyment of your relationship or marriage with your Queen? Is your low self-esteem holding you back and stopping you from achieving the success in your relationship that you desire? Having a natural, healthy, abundant sense of self-esteem is critical to both your happiness and success in life, however if you suffer from low self-esteem, then these feelings have probably been built up gradually over several years, and they can seem like a burden and hindrance to your happiness with your Queen.

Your affirmations are going to help you to get deep inside your subconscious. When targeted at your mind in the right way, affirmations can make dramatic changes to the way you see yourself and to your self-esteem. Some of the changes you will witness almost immediately include seeing yourself differently. Additionally, you will focus on the positives in your personality and you will appreciate your talents and abilities. Just shifting into a more positive attitude will change the way you view yourself and improve your self-esteem. This will lead you to get so much more out of life and everything you do. You will start to naturally project a warm, modest confidence in your interactions with your Queen.

Rather than reacting to her out of fear, worry, and self-doubt, you will be proactive, and every action you take will come from a sense of subtle, natural self-confidence. You will be more lighthearted, and you will accept yourself for who you are. With this new attitude, you will easily deal with your limitations openly instead of negatively. You will begin to accept that you deserve a strong loving Queen, and you deserve to be able to worship her freely instead of being chained by past patriarchal conditioning. Your focus in life will change.

Instead of dwelling on the past, you will begin to accept it and everything that has happened to you. You will be able to let go and focus on being present with your Queen. You will feel excited about the future and all of the possibilities open to you right now. You will be much less concerned with other people's opinions of you. Your self-image will not be built by other people anymore. Instead of measuring yourself against others, or even taking their negative feedback to heart and letting it shape your personality, you will start to build your sense of self-esteem yourself—based on your positive opinions of yourself and of your abilities. All of this translates to a much more rewarding experience, more intimacy with your Queen, and a deeper, more fulfilling relationship or marriage.

I give my heart to my Queen, and I am ready to receive her love.
(Repeat 4 Times)

I love my Queen more than I ever thought possible.
(Repeat 4 Times)

My Queen is my soulmate. I desire no other.

(Repeat 4 Times)

My Queen and I have deep, passionate love.

(Repeat 4 Times)

I am in a wonderful relationship with my Queen.

(Repeat 4 Times)

I deserve love and affection from a great woman.

(Repeat 4 Times)

I love who I am, and my Queen accepts me, as I accept her.

(Repeat 4 Times)

I am worthy of a healthy, loving relationship.

(Repeat 4 Times)

I deserve to be happy in my relationship.

(Repeat 4 Times)

I love myself, and I love my Queen.

(Repeat 4 Times)

I am in the healthiest relationship of my life!

(Repeat 4 Times)

I have mind-blowing passion in my relationship with my Queen.

(Repeat 4 Times)

The Universe is bringing more romance and passion to me and my Queen.

(Repeat 4 Times)

I am happy to give and receive love every day!

(Repeat 4 Times)

I am in a relationship with a Queen who I respect and who also respects me.

(Repeat 4 Times)

Love starts with me.

(Repeat 4 Times)

I am love and light.

(Repeat 4 Times)

I am enough, and I am worthy.

(Repeat 4 Times)

The more I love my Queen, the more she loves me in return.

(Repeat 4 Times)

My relationship is always fulfilling.

(Repeat 4 Times)

I am grateful for the love in my life.

(Repeat 4 Times)

Sharing love comes easily to me.

(Repeat 4 Times)

General Relationship Affirmations

My relationship is a positive, loving experience.
(Repeat 4 Times)

I am worthy of love and deserve to receive love in abundance.
(Repeat 4 Times)

I love those around me, and I love myself.
(Repeat 4 Times)

My Queen and I are both happy and in love. Our relationship is joyous.
(Repeat 4 Times)

I am thankful for the love in my life, and I am thankful for my Queen.
(Repeat 4 Times)

I only attract healthy, loving relationships.
(Repeat 4 Times)

I happily give and receive love each day.

(Repeat 4 Times)

Each day I am so grateful for how loved I am and much people care about me.

(Repeat 4 Times)

I open my heart to love and know that I deserve it.

(Repeat 4 Times)

I deserve to receive the love I get, and I open myself to the love the Queen gives me.

(Repeat 4 Times)

My love and our relationship grows stronger every day.

(Repeat 4 Times)

I am capable and deserving of a long-lasting relationship.

(Repeat 4 Times)

My relationship will be open, honest, and full of abundance.

(Repeat 4 Times)

Love surrounds me.

(Repeat 4 Times)

I exhale negativity and inhale happiness.

(Repeat 4 Times)

Today I continue to create the foundation of a happy and loving relationship.

(Repeat 4 Times)

Happiness begins with me. I have the power to create my own happiness.

(Repeat 4 Times)

I let go of my past conditioning and look to the future.

(Repeat 4 Times)

CHAPTER 15

Your Cuckolding Submission Affirmations

C uckolding is growing in popularity. Google shows that 200,000 people a month search cuckolding and many couples are interested in it. But cuckolding is controversial, and I feel that it is the one part of female led life that men have the most hesitation with. It is understandable, cuckolding involves getting turned on by their Queen having sex with someone else.

You will watch your woman with a third, well-endowed man. More women are choosing to add this to their sex lives and their men are supportive, but many are having a very hard time committing. So, let's expose some of the myths.

First, cuckolding is not a necessary part of Female Led Relationships. Couples engage in cuckolding only if it is something you both agree on. Second, cuckolding does not involve cheating. Unlike cheating and infidelity, cuckolding demands the consent of both people and often it is done together. Cheating is sneaking around behind your partner's back and having sex or a relationship with an outside person. Men accept cheating, and according to statistics, at least 60 percent of all men will engage in cheating. Not all men engage in cheating, but you can agree that it happens.

How many times have you found yourself flirting with another woman or spending more time with a female co-worker or friend? How many times are you watching porn or other women naked having sex? Men will argue that watching porn is not cheating, but in the Female Led Relationship world, any attention you spend in a sexual manner that is not devoted to your Queen's pleasure is unacceptable. So, cuckolding presents the elegant solution to if you are a man who is unable to satisfy the Queen due to erectile dysfunction, or you're too small or you spend too much time masturbating.

Psychologists have suggested that there may be a biological urge referred to as the "sperm competition theory" that may play a role in the desire for men to engage in cuckolding. Watching another man satisfy your woman can wake up the body, increasing the need to have longer and more orgasms. Other reasons for men's desire to engage in cuckolding is compersion, which is the desire to see your Queen happy and getting sexually satisfied makes you even happier and turned on. In addition, men enjoy cuckolding because it is the ultimate sign of submission. You submit completely to your Queen when you support her desire to be with the Bull and have your complete support.

How you go about cuckolding is explained in my book *Cuckolding,* and you and your Queen are encouraged to read it. But with respect to affirmations, they will help you to accept and become comfortable with allowing your Queen to engage in cuckolding without feelings of jealousy, fear, or anger. Cuckolding is still something you will do together and requires your consent. But many men feel pressured to be happy with it, but deep down inside they reject it. Cuckolding affirmations can help you to get past these feelings of resentment if this is what you and your Queen desires.

I accept my Queen's decision to engage with a Bull.
(Repeat 4 Times)

I submit to my Queen's desire to be with another man, and I will participate as she commands.
(Repeat 4 Times)

My Queen makes the decisions about cuckolding, but I support anything she decides to do as she is my supreme ruler.

(Repeat 4 Times)

I accept the man, who is the Bull, as simply adding excitement to my Queen and my sex life.

(Repeat 4 Times)

I am number one in my Queen's life even if we decide together to do cuckolding.

(Repeat 4 Times)

My Queen's love for me remains the most important part of our relationship.

(Repeat 4 Times)

I allow my Queen the freedom to explore, and I support her desire to get satisfaction in any way she chooses.

(Repeat 4 Times)

My Queen loves me above all others.

(Repeat 4 Times)

Cuckolding is something my Queen and I will accept together and I am free to discuss my concerns.

(Repeat 4 Times)

I welcome my opportunity to pleasure my Queen after she engages with her Bull, if it is what she desires.

(Repeat 4 Times)

I am first in my Queen's life above everyone else, no matter what we decide to do for excitement and stimulation.

(Repeat 4 Times)

CHAPTER 16

History of Goddess Worship

As we have seen, affirmations help with reprogramming your past conditioning and helps with your acceptance of your Queen as supreme. But worshipping your woman and placing her on a pedestal is not new. Goddess worship has existed for centuries, and it was made popular in the 70s with spiritual beliefs or practices. The term "Goddess" refers to a local or specific deity linked clearly to a particular culture and often to particular aspects, attributes, and powers.

Greek and Roman mythology had several female goddesses, as did most of the ancient pagan faiths. Indigenous faiths around the world worshiped countless female goddesses, too.

The movement grew as a reaction to perceptions of predominant organized religion as male-dominated. Female sacred images are associated with some of the oldest archaeological evidence for religious expression, and they still have efficacy in the contemporary world. Archaeologists have interpreted artifacts excavated from "Old Europe" points to societies of Neolithic Europe that were goddess-centered worshipping a female deity. Goddess images are depicted in a wide range of forms, from aniconic representations, such as abstract organs of reproduction, to fully elaborated icons decorated with the finery of monarchy. They are linked to all major aspects of life, including birth, initiation, marriage, reproduction, and death.

Sculptured images and cave paintings of female figures excavated in hundreds of Upper Paleolithic sites throughout Europe and northern Asia, including France, Spain, Italy, Germany, Austria, the Ukraine, and Siberia. These images, carved in bone, stone, antler, and mammoth tusks, outnumber those of male figures ten to one, and they are some of the earliest archaeological evidence. Many of these have been discovered Aurignacian deposits as old as thirty to forty thousand years. However, they appear more frequently about 25,000 years ago.

Remarkably, these same goddess figurines have been discovered from sites dated as late as the early Neolithic period. One of the earliest of these figurines, found in the Dordogne region of France, was estimated to be thirty-two thousand years old, roughly the age of the famous cave art of that period and situated one level above the Neanderthal artifacts associated with what are believed to be ceremonial burials. This "pregnant" figure was carved from reindeer antler and is marked by a series of small notches that do not appear to be purely decorative. Goddess worship has played a central role in the worldwide transition from small-scale social organization to the emergence of civilizations in India, the ancient Near East, Greece, Rome, China, and Japan. In these complex agricultural societies, female deities have been variously linked to the fertility of crops, the sovereignty of kingship, the protection of urban ceremonial centers, and the waging of warfare against enemies.

No civilization in the world developed goddess worship so elaborately as India with so many famous figurines of mother goddesses found in the Indus Valley, dated at 2500 to 1500 BCE, along with abstract stone rings representing the yoni and lingam, prototypes for the later god Śiva and his female consort. A great deal of modern Hinduism also swivels around the idea of a feminine aspect to the universe, with the creation goddess Shakti being one of the faith's three most powerful forces—the "activity in all things, the great power that creates and destroys, the primordial essence, the womb from which all things proceed and into which all things return."

Goddess worship emerges as a somewhat separate cult in Hinduism and eventually in Tibetan Buddhism. This goddess worship was particularly strong in eastern India where it continues to flourish today. A number of goddesses were prominent in ancient Egypt: Nut, goddess of the sky and consort of the earth god, Geb; the goddess Neith, patroness of victorious weapons and the art of weaving; Isis, goddess of wisdom; and Hathor, another sky goddess who assumed various forms. Some of these goddesses were deeply entwined in the development and continuity of divine kingship.

The name Isis is related to the term for "chair" or "throne." The throne or "holy seat" of the pharaoh was the "mother of the king." The pharaohs thought themselves to be sons of Isis. Later, Isis became linked to the female god Osiris. The heroic story depicts Isis's famous search for her murdered husband's corpse, her discovery of it, and his resurrection. Eventually Isis became universalized as a benevolent goddess of the harvest. Her cult spread from Egypt to Greece and throughout the Roman Empire.

In ancient Sumer, Mesopotamia, considered the oldest civilization in world history, the goddess Nidaba also known as Nisaba was given credit for the invention of clay tablets and the art of writing. Nidaba was considered the "Goddess of wisdom" and the great teacher who gave advice everywhere, including endowing the king with wisdom. An ancient hymn states: "Nisaba, the woman radiant with joy, faithful woman, scribe, lady who knows everything guided your fingers onto the clay, embellished the writing on the tablets, made the hand resplendent with the golden stylus, the measuring rod, the gleaming surveyor's line, the cubit ruler which gives wisdom Nisaba lavishly bestowed on you." Nisaba was also the deity who made cities possible: "The place which you do not establish, there humankind is not established, cities are not built."

The earliest examples of writing so far discovered were business accounts in the Temple of the Queen of Heaven in Erech in ancient Sumer. In India, the goddess Sarasvatia was the inventor of the original alphabet. The world's oldest texts on cuneiform clay tablets were discovered after having been buried for at least four thousand years. Some of these texts tell the life story of Inanna from adolescence through womanhood and her eventual apotheosis. The texts are extremely rich; they reveal the sexual fears and desires of the goddess, an elaborate history of kinship among various deities in her family tree, her power as queen of Sumer, and her responsibilities for the redistribution of resources and fertility of the earth.

In 390-0 to 3500 BCE, the oldest shrine of Uruk was dedicated to Inanna, as were numerous later temples. She was the supreme patroness of the city. The goddess Inanna, who was most likely derived from Neolithic and possibly even earlier Paleolithic roots, played the principal role in the religious tradition of an urban society. She was considered to have equal status with the sky god. In these ancient civilizations, they believe that women were viewed as equal even supreme compared to men. So, femininity has always been an integral part of religion, and indeed of civilization. Many scholars have argued that the earliest civilizations could have been matriarchal. Goddess spirituality, goddess worship, the sacred feminine, and the feminine divine all refer to a deity most often identified as "Mother Goddess" or the "Great Goddess." Other names used include Mother Earth, Gaia, Sophia, Artemis, Diana, and Isis. Often associated with the earth, the moon, and fertility, the goddess is usually described as an energy force inside every living and nonliving thing. What lies behind the allure of goddess worship, especially those women who feel marginalized or devalued by what they perceive as the traditional, male-dominated church—its appeal is found in its affirmation of female spirituality.

Masculine and feminine are energies, not just biological genders. Every man has some masculine and some feminine energy, and so does every woman. The balance we seek is not only between men and women, but between the masculine and feminine energy, which are to be found everywhere in life. The feminine way is not inferior, as we had deemed it for thousands of years, but it is different. Through a synergy of masculine and feminine strengths, we find the emergence of a whole that is far greater and the sum of it to individual parts. This is what Female Led Relationships do—it allows the blending of feminine and masculine perfectly. Men can do several positive things to support a female led lifestyle. First, women have been disenfranchised for thousands of years. Feminine energy has been given very little respect, and we have all lost out as a result.

The first step is embracing change. *Love and Obey* affirmations are a giant step toward change for men. The second step is for man to fully release past conditioning that has affected the relationship to women and caused men to dishonor women. The third step is for man to embrace and recognize feminine energy, her beauty, her capacity to love, her laughter, her freedom to feel and express emotion. Man can discover and then learn to worship the feminine face of the divine. *Love and Obey* affirmations can support men's transition from patriarchal to female led life.

CHAPTER 17

Journey To Real Submission

There is a reason that ancient civilizations erected statues of women almost guiding us on how to worship correctly. When you learn the rules of worship, you embark on the journey to real submission. At the essence of every woman's heart is the divine feminine. It contains everything that has ever been beautiful, or lovely, or inspiring, in any woman, anywhere, at any time. The very essence of every woman's heart is the peak of wisdom, the peak of inspiration, the peak of sexual desirability, the peak of soothing, healing love. The peak of everything. But it's protected, for good reason, by many walls that a man must get through. As you are able to get through the walls with your daily affirmations, it intensifies your capacity for devotion, and as you do so, you are rewarded with the love and attention of your Queen.

When you view one of these statues, you begin your journey on the outside just looking at her beauty. This is similar to dating and getting to know your Queen. You are on the outside until you begin to focus on going deeper. Some relationships remain at this point for years. Couples just exist in what appears to be a solid relationship until problems and disagreements begin to destroy it. But a relationship that is stuck at the outer level cannot withstand challenges. Like entering the walls of the statue, you must go in deeper. Just focusing and showing your commitment to your Queen daily takes you to the next level. As you move through her walls, she opens her heart to you.

She'll share with you her insecurities, her desires, and her dreams. Some men can become uneasy at this point and in Female Led Relationships, this is the point where men tend to allow their patriarchal conditioning to take hold. They are unable to submit, and it begins to cause issues for them. At this point, you are a "fake sub". You are trying to submit but unable to fully release past conditioning. When the Queen senses the hesitation, this can make the relationship decline fast. Your affirmations help you to release and submit completely. They focus your goals and devotions on what's important, and they help to alleviate the stress of going deeper. This is how you make that transition to "Real Sub" or real submission.

A "Fake Sub" or fake submissive is a man who pretends to enjoy Female Led Relationships only for the superficial aspects of being with a powerful woman who can dominate him. A "Real Sub" or real submissive is a man who takes this journey into deeper and deeper worship of his Queen. Like visiting the ancient Goddess statues when you get to the center, you gain the ultimate reward of complete love of your Queen. You discover the very essence of the feminine. When you love a woman completely, at the very essence of her being, you connect with her divine. This transforms your relationship or marriage into the ultimate female led experience. You help your Queen to be all that she can be, and in return, she helps you to be the best supportive gentleman you can be.

As you have just experienced for yourself, my erotic *Love & Obey* Female Led Affirmations are helping men to eliminate all their patriarchal conditioning, selfishness, and male ego while reprogramming their mind to accept female led and the Queen's position as supreme leader. Changing past conditioning takes a lot of patience, practice, and time. The key to this journey is consistent practice and reinforcing the rules of worship. Affirmations are powerful messages that are absorbed into the subconscious. Suddenly you are operating from a much different place. Together with your Queen, affirmations help to deepen your devotion to her and accelerates your submissive training. Most men think that it is possible to just start a Female Led Relationship, and while it can be fun in the beginning, only when you get to deeper levels of submission can you really experience the power of being the supportive gentleman to a powerful, dominant Queen who enjoys taking the lead.

Many male subs have sexual fantasies about submission to a dominant female, but many of these men are not willing to do anything other than fulfill their female dominant sexual fantasies. As a result, any sexual fantasies that their Queen desires are simply dismissed. This is male selfishness, and it stems from patriarchal conditioning that cannot be released. "Fake Subs" seek a dominant woman that can fulfill their sexual fantasies without fulfilling hers. These "Fake Subs" don't want to perform household chores, run errands, and serve the Queen in everyday life. They simply want to fulfill their own selfish sexual fantasies. So, while many men think they are submissive, they are actually not submissive to the wishes of their dominant female. This is important because submitting to your Queen for your own selfish desires will result in power struggles later on and an inability for you to accept her command fully. A good example are sissies who believe that by wearing women's clothing that this is enough to be submissive. This does not necessarily qualify as submission, and it is a very common error made in these types

Marisa Rudder

of relationships. A *Love and Obey* man is still strong and powerful in his own life. He can hold a commanding position and be a leader in all aspects of his life, but he can still be submissive to his Queen and serve her desires. A Real Sub is really this type of man. He accepts the Queen's lead and can offer her the support she needs as a supportive gentleman.

Love and Obey affirmations help you reprogram this conditioning that is holding you back from experiencing more love and happiness you and your Queen deserves. Men crave female leadership in relationships because of increased intimacy of giving up control and experiencing a woman taking control, the amazing power exchange that happens in a *Love & Obey* Female Led Relationship is addictive. Many men think submitting to a woman is the most intimate act they have ever experienced, and they feel honored to submit. Many couples enter the *Love and Obey* world because they want to spice up their sex life with paddles, leather corsets, and blindfolds. They start out by role-playing as a sexy dominatrix with their husband. This is encouraged, but female led life must transition from the bedroom to daily life for it to be truly powerful and life-changing.

Why do female led women have no trouble attracting and keeping any man they want? Why is it that some of these powerful women can easily get their man to commit? Why is it that some women know how to get what they truly want from their man? These female led women understand something about men, which a majority have no idea about. You, as the supportive gentleman, must now move yourself from the fringes to becoming her real submissive because that's what she needs. Strong women are self-sufficient and they don't need a man who is on the fence. By fully committing to the female led lifestyle and treating her like a Queen, releasing past patriarchal conditioning, and accepting her as your supreme leader, you catapult yourself into being the most important person in her life.

In relationships, strong women do not view you as a means to an end—a way to become more financially or emotionally stable, or to cure themselves of loneliness, etc. They don't have any ulterior motive to being with you, so you don't have to worry. There's a lot more security in a relationship with a strong woman because you don't have to walk on eggshells around her to keep her happy. You don't have to bring home a six-figure income to keep her satisfied, and you don't have to babysit her emotions. Because of this, they don't approach relationships the same way those who are just wading in the dating pool might. They dive right in and know their target long before they've even hit the water.

In other words, these women know what to look for in a mate. They don't seek out a partner to get anything out of them; they seek someone in order to add value to their life.

They only want someone who will lift them up, not drag them down. In the same way, they also wish to add meaning to someone else's life, and see the importance of both give and take in a relationship. A strong woman would never take more than she's willing to give when it comes to love. In a relationship with a strong woman, things are dealt with in an adult manner, with respect and grace. These types of women don't let their emotions get the best of them and always listen to their partner's point of view without interrupting. Strong women say no when they don't feel that deep inner emotional urge to be with a man. When there isn't enough attraction, she will always pull away sooner or later.

So, is there something you can do to change her mind? The answer is absolutely. Yes. Do you know that it's very simple to give a strong woman that inner gut feeling which tells her that you are the only one for her? And how you do that is by becoming her ultimate supportive gentleman making it your mission and life purpose, to ensure her happiness. The harsh fact is that 95 percent of the men out there will never have the kind of success they desire with women. Most men are clueless when it comes to women. They rely on luck because they don't know what to do. And even worse, they make no real effort to work on this area of their life. They live in the false idea that someday they're going to magically find the woman of their dreams and life will be smooth. But it doesn't work this way.

Nothing will work out by itself. Success with a strong female led woman boils down to having the skills on what actions to take. And unless you have those skills, you will always struggle.

Today women are now somewhat freer to assert their dominance over men, and men cannot resist a strong woman. Furthermore, many men welcome discipline from their Queens. Strong women are seen as exciting and anything can happen. Bad girls are the ones who will throw a man down, tie him up, strip off his pants, and tease him till he can't stand it anymore. Who can resist giving up all of the power to a sexy, dominant woman who is fully capable of taking charge? Also, an unstable hierarchy can cause men considerable anxiety, but an established chain of command, such as that practiced by the military and many workplaces, reduces testosterone and curbs male aggression. When a man knows his Queen is in charge and agrees, he will be calmer and easier to deal with.

In *Psychology Today,* after looking into the mating preferences of more than 5,000 men and women by way of survey, researcher and biological anthropologist Helen Fisher, PhD, writes that men desire smart, strong, successful women. And 87 percent of men said they would date a woman who was more intellectual than they were, who was better educated, and who made considerably more money than they did, while 86 percent said they were in search of a woman who was confident and self-assured.

Strong women go after the things they want in life. They don't sit by and just wait for love to fall into their lap. They're not afraid to flirt and show a true interest, but they also define that interest. They let a man know right away if they're looking for a simple hookup or if they're after a real relationship, and they don't stick around if a guy wants something different. Men don't have to guess with strong women, and they can sit back and let her make the first move and take control. This is the opposite of most other areas of life where they must compete. With a woman in charge, they are free to allow her to lead and make decisions. This also makes the woman happier, and a happier woman is a much sexier woman. A Female Led Relationship does not make men less powerful.

It actually can empower men much more than in a traditional male-led relationship because the man is motivated to become the key supporter of a woman. He becomes the central focus of her life as much as she is the center of his. But your Queen will trigger what psychologist James Bauer says is something deep with her guy. Something he wants more than love and even more than the hero instinct. Men have a biological drive to feel needed, to feel important, and to provide for the woman he cares about.

There are many reasons your Queen desires a Female Led Relationship and why she wants you to fully submit to your role as a supportive gentleman. Here are some reasons why women would seek out a FLR:

1. She wants to take the lead and make decisions and changes when it comes to the household and their family.

2. She desires less power struggle, making it easier for her to be relaxed and at peace with you.

3. She can deepen her love and because she feels that she will get the care, attention, and respect she deserves as an equal.

4. She enjoys the power to control every part of the relationship.

She may want to feel that she is in a better position to help you to change.

CHAPTER 18

Writing Your Own Personalized Affirmations

Writing your own affirmations script is not as difficult as you think. Even if you do not consider yourself a writer, anyone can write an effective affirmation by simply following a few of my rules and techniques. My first suggestion is that if you are going to be stating the *Love & Obey* Female Led Affirmations in your partnership, you should be the one who writes the affirmation. If you write the affirmation, you can focus on the words and your personal goals of submitting to your loving female authority. You should be focused on the meaning and effect of the words.

You can choose to write affirmations together with your Queen and make this something you both commit to. Feel free to modify any of my suggested affirmations to make them more personal. Your mind is a powerful thing. Once you fill it with positive thoughts, your life will start to change. When you remind yourself of your relationship goals through affirmations every single day, though, you ensure that you are acting in the direction of your goals every single day. You get inspired by tapping into the feeling of empowerment and self-belief that affirmations can create. And you start projecting the energy to the world, and the confidence to yourself, that you are ready to achieve these goals. Words can literally change our brains.

Here are some basic rules to remember when writing affirmations: Use present tense, use positivity, make them believable, and make sure they are deeply personal and reflect how you truly feel. Write your affirmations in such a way that they focus on what you want in your Female Led Relationship, rather than what you are trying to avoid or eliminate from your life. Think about how good you will feel when you achieve your goals, and how good it feels to know that positive changes are taking place. Add affirmations that describe these positive feelings of success.

Great leaders have used the power of words to transform our emotions, to enlist us in their causes, and to shape the course of destiny. When Winston Churchill spoke of "their finest hour" or when Martin Luther King, Jr. described his "dream," we clearly saw that their beliefs were formed by words—and that they could also be changed by words. But what about our own ability to use words to ignite change, to move ourselves to action, and to improve the quality of our lives? We all know words provide us with a vehicle for expressing and sharing experiences with others. But do you realize that the words you habitually choose also affect how your brain reacts on a physiological level?

Words can affect our brain and how we perceive the world and our circumstances. Science shows us that negative words that suggest everything is a catastrophe, such as "We will never recover from this," or "This is a complete disaster," can negatively affect our mental and emotional health while positive words can have positive benefits. Over time, our mind believes what we are saying to ourselves. Optimistic words condition us to see a brighter future. And negative ones keep us stuck. They can enable us to have a more or less constructive and resourceful viewpoint, and they can also influence our resilience or our ability to bounce back after difficulties. Positive words build resilience and calm the body. Negative ones generate fear. Our internal narrative also affects how we communicate with others, which in turn influences how those around us feel about their lives and future. Put another way, when we use positive words like "love" and "peace," we can alter how our brain functions by increasing cognitive reasoning and strengthening areas in our frontal lobes. Using positive words more often than negative ones can kick-start the motivational centers of the brain, propelling them into action.

Likewise, when we use negative words, we're keeping certain neuro-chemicals from being produced, which contribute to stress management. As humans, we're hardwired to worry. It's how our primal brain protects us from dangerous situations for survival. Words are the vehicle for change and inspiration and allow the brightest minds on Earth to free themselves of the chains in their minds. Words turn dreams and visions into reality and give life to all that remains hidden and kept away.

They allow ideas, innovations, and movements to see the light of day when in any other circumstance they would have stayed asleep in the midst of chaotic humdrum in our minds. Being positive isn't about pretending things are fantastic when they are not. That is delusion. But it is about being open to and looking forward to things getting better. Negativity generates internal stress in the body and a feeling of hopelessness. This adversely affects motivation. Positive thinking reduces our heart rate and enables us to recover from anxiety more easily. Even one negative word triggers fear and all the sensations that come with that. Researchers monitored subjects' brain responses to auditory and imagined negative words. During this process, she discovered painful or negative words increase Implicit Processing within the subgenual anterior cingulate cortex . Their study proved that negative words release stress and anxiety-inducing hormones in subjects.

Dr. Andrew Newberg, a neuroscientist at Thomas Jefferson University, and Mark Robert Waldman, a communications expert, state, "A single word has the power to influence the expression of genes that regulate physical and emotional stress." They believed that exercising positive thoughts can quite literally change one's reality. They also state, "By holding a positive and optimistic word in your mind, you stimulate frontal lobe activity. This area includes specific language centers that connect directly to the motor cortex responsible for moving you into action. And as our research has shown, the longer you concentrate on positive words, the more you begin to affect other areas of the brain." Over time, given sustained positive thoughts, functions in the parietal lobe start to change. Consequently, this alters our perception of the self and those around us. Essentially, holding a positive view of ourselves helps train our brain to see the good in others.

Thus, by exercising consistent positive thoughts and speech, we not only change our self-perception, but how we perceive the world around us. Our thought patterns directly shape our perception of the world and those around us. Our thoughts become our words, and therefore our language.

Newberg and Waldman also state, "Functions in the parietal lobe start to change, which changes your perception of yourself and the people you interact with. A positive view of yourself will bias you toward seeing the good in others, whereas a negative self-image will include you toward suspicion and doubt. Over time the structure of your thalamus will also change in response to your conscious words, thoughts, and feelings, and we believe that the thalamic changes affect the way in which you perceive reality."

According to Sonja Lyubomirsky, one of the world's leading researchers on happiness, if you want to develop lifelong satisfaction, you should regularly engage in positive thinking about yourself and do so by sharing your happiest events with others through language. If you use your words, and your inner dialogues and conversations with others, to engage in optimism and positivity, you'll find yourself moving in a more life-enhancing direction.

While external consequences of language have been observable throughout history, we have only recently acquired tools such as fMRI, EEG, PET, MEG, NIRS, CT and eye tracking that enable us to see how language reaches back to shape the brain itself. We now know that experience with multiple languages can produce extensive changes to our neural architecture that are observable across the lifespan and across domains: from infancy to old age, from sensory perception to higher cognitive processing. Using and learning language can change our very biology, thereby confirming the ancient intuition that words can, in fact, alter physical reality.

Bilinguals also have increased white matter in the tracts connecting frontal control areas to posterior and subcortical sensory and motor regions, which may allow them to off-load some of the work to areas that handle more procedural activities. Increased gray and white matter, as well as the ability to flexibly recruit different brain regions, may help explain why bilingualism can ward off dementia for several years. How you decide to use your affirmations is completely up to you. Feel free to experiment. You can start with doing them alone, then invite your Queen to do it together with you. Remember this is a tool designed to help reprogram past conditioning that is limiting you from fully submitting to serve your Queen. The experience is important, and so are your words, visualizations, rituals, and anything else, including soft music, which can enhance your experience.

Conclusion

Female Led Relationships are on the rise but change in relationships or marriages can be challenging. When men decide to submit fully to their Queen, the desire is strong and often that is the driving force for Female Led Relationships, but settling into daily life and countering past conditioning can be an issue for many. There can be a constant battle. Patriarchal thinking and rigid gender roles can prevent some men from being able to be their best in a Female Led Relationship. When men can fully commit and follow their Queen's lead, all is well. He experiences tremendous relief and generally he is much happier.

Love and Obey affirmations require daily practice, but they help to reprogram past conditioning. Affirmations have been proven to work, and strong scientific research studies support their efficacy. Much work has been done on neuroplasticity and psychology with the results to be very positive for the use of affirmations to bring about great transformation.

Affirmations may be used during sex or alone, and there are many different types, as well as writing personalized ones directed at the areas you wish to change.

Patriarchal conditioning has been an accepted part of our society, but support for it is dwindling since it has been shown to be rigid and does not support today's female led world. Men are eager to release patriarchal conditioning as they accept the leadership of their Queen. Affirmations are a powerful way to explore spiritual and Tantric sex, deepening the experience. What is important is that men who have submitted and made the decision to serve their Queen must practice affirmations daily and release past conditioning. This represents the journey from fake sub to real sub, but when your transformation has been successful, you will experience joy, love, and happiness in your relationship with your Queen on a whole new level. Men's acceptance of their responsibility in changing the patriarchal mindset and accepting women as their leaders will help to spearhead the female led movement, which is already growing leaps and bounds. Men, submit to your Queen.

THE END

www.ingramcontent.com/pod-product-compliance
Lightning Source LLC
Chambersburg PA
CBHW021235090426
42740CB00006B/541